Praise for *The Courage to Be Disliked*

"Marie Kondo, but for your brain."

—HelloGiggles

"Adlerian psychology meets Stoic philosophy in Socratic dialogue. Compelling from front to back. Highly recommend."

—Marc Andreessen, venture capitalist and founder of Andreessen Horowitz

"A nuanced discussion of a complex theory, with moments of real philosophical insight . . . [It's] refreshing and useful to read a philosophy that goes against many contemporary orthodoxies. More than a century since Adler founded his school of psychology, there's still insight and novelty in his theories."

—Quartzy

"[*The Courage to be Disliked* guides] readers toward achieving happiness and lasting change . . . For those seeking a discourse that helps explain who they are in the world, Kishimi and Koga provide an illuminating conversation."

—*Library Journal*

ALSO BY ICHIRO KISHIMI
AND FUMITAKE KOGA

The Courage to Be Disliked

THE
COURAGE
TO BE
HAPPY

✦

Discover the Power of
Positive Psychology and Choose
Happiness Every Day

✦

ICHIRO KISHIMI
AND
FUMITAKE KOGA

ATRIA PAPERBACK
New York London Toronto Sydney New Delhi

ATRIA
PAPERBACK

An Imprint of Simon & Schuster, LLC
1230 Avenue of the Americas
New York, NY 10020

First published in Japan as *Shiawase Ni Naru Yuki* by Diamond Inc., Tokyo in 2016

English translation first published in Australia in 2019 by Allen & Unwin

This English edition published by arrangement with Diamond Inc. c/o Tuttle-Mori Agency Inc., Tokyo, through Chandler Crawford Agency Inc., Massachusetts, USA

First Atria Paperback edition May 2024

ATRIA PAPERBACK and colophon are trademarks of Simon & Schuster, LLC

Simon & Schuster: Celebrating 100 Years of Publishing in 2024

For information about special discounts for bulk purchases, please contact Simon & Schuster Special Sales at 1-866-506-1949 or business@simonandschuster.com.

The Simon & Schuster Speakers Bureau can bring authors to your live event. For more information or to book an event, contact the Simon & Schuster Speakers Bureau at 1-866-248-3049 or visit our website at www.simonspeakers.com.

Manufactured in the United States of America

1 3 5 7 9 10 8 6 4 2

Library of Congress Cataloging-in-Publication Data

Names: Kishimi, Ichiro, 1956– author. | Koga, Fumitake, 1973– author.
Title: The courage to be happy : discover the power of positive psychology and choose happiness every day / Ichiro Kishimi and Fumitake Koga.
Other titles: Shiawase ni naru yuki. English
Description: New York, NY : Atria Books, 2019. | "First published in Japan in 2016 by Diamond Inc., Tokyo as Shiawase Ni Naru Yuki." |
Identifiers: LCCN 2019019172 (print) | LCCN 2019021615 (ebook) | ISBN 9781982123024 (eBook) | ISBN 9781982123000 (hardcover)
Subjects: LCSH: Adler, Alfred, 1870–1937. | Adlerian psychology. | Happiness. | Self-actualization (Psychology)
Classification: LCC BF175.5.A33 (ebook) | LCC BF175.5.A33 K5713 2019 (print) | DDC 150.19/53—dc23
LC record available at https://lccn.loc.gov_2019019172

ISBN 978-1-9821-2300-0
ISBN 978-1-6680-6600-3 (pbk)
ISBN 978-1-9821-2302-4 (ebook)

Contents

Contents

PART II

Why Negate Reward and Punishment?

PART III

From the Principle of Competition to the Principle of Cooperation

PART IV

Give, and It Shall Be Given Unto You

PART V

Choose a Life You Love

THE
COURAGE
TO BE
HAPPY

Authors' Note

Alfred Adler, the thinker who was a hundred years ahead of his time. Though he stands beside Sigmund Freud and Carl Gustav Jung as one of the most important figures in the world of psychology, Adler was for many years a "forgotten giant." Since the publication of *The Courage to Be Disliked*, the context of Adler and his school of thought has gone through a remarkable transformation. Adler has been widely known in Europe and America for some time. But now, after our book spent a record-setting fifty-one weeks as a number-one bestseller—having sold millions of copies in South Korea and Japan—I have a strong sense that Adler is present within many people, and no longer needs introduction. There is something deeply moving about his ideals being accepted in Asia after the passage of a hundred years.

The Courage to Be Disliked is a kind of map for informing people of the existence of Adlerian psychology, and for giving an overview of Adler's ideas. It is a grand map that we put together over the course of several years, with the intention of creating a definitive introduction to Adlerian psychology.

The Courage to Be Happy, on the other hand, is a kind of compass for actually putting Adler's ideas into practice and leading a happy life. And it may also be thought of as a collection of behavioral guidelines showing how one may progress toward the objectives laid out in the first book.

In *The Courage to Be Happy*, once more we find the philosopher engaged in a dialogue with the pessimistic youth. Three years after the conclusion of *The Courage to Be Disliked*, the youth, who has become a teacher with the intention of putting Adler's ideas into practice, calls on the philosopher one last time. Frustrated with Adlerian psychology and angry with the philosopher for introducing him to Adler's ideals, the youth has returned to the philosopher's study to challenge everything the philosopher taught him and insist that he cease to corrupt other young minds with ideals that don't hold up in the real world when interacting with real people. Calmly, the philosopher invites the youth to join him for one final conversation about having courage not only to take the first step toward happiness, but to continue walking along the path of self-improvement in order to love, be self-reliant, and nurture community feeling.

In what way can we make concrete progress on the path to happiness shown in the preceding volume, *The Courage to Be Disliked?* How can we put Adlerian psychology into practice in our everyday lives? And what is that conclusion arrived at by Adler, "the biggest choice in life," that everyone must make in order to live in happiness?

The curtain opens once more on this strong-medicine philosophical dialogue. Do you have the *courage* to climb the stairway of understanding with the youth?

It should have been a more lighthearted and friendly visit. "I hope you will not mind if, at some point, I visit you here again. Yes, as an irreplaceable friend. And I won't be saying anything more about taking part in your arguments." Indeed, the youth had blurted out such words on his departure that day. Now, however, three years had gone by, and he had arrived at this man's study with completely different intentions. The youth was trembling with the gravity of what he was about to confess, and he felt at a loss as to where to begin.

Introduction

People Misunderstand Adler's Ideas

PHILOSOPHER: Please, tell me, what is going on?

YOUTH: You're asking why I have come to this study again? Well, unfortunately, I'm not here for a simple visit and to rekindle an old friendship. I'm sure you are busy, as am I. So, naturally, there is a pressing issue that has brought me here once more.

PHILOSOPHER: Yes, of course, it would seem so.

YOUTH: I have thought things over. I have worried and obsessed over it all more than is necessary and reexamined everything completely. In doing so, I arrived at a very serious conclusion, and decided to come here to convey it to you. I know you have much to do, but please give me a moment of your time for just this one evening. Because this will probably be my final visit.

PHILOSOPHER: What happened?

YOUTH: . . . You haven't figured it out? It's the problem I've been suffering over for so long: "Do I give up on Adler or not?"

PHILOSOPHER: Ah. I see.

YOUTH: I'll get right to the point: Adler's ideas are a farce. An utter farce. Actually, I have to go further, and say that they are dangerous, even harmful ideas. While you yourself are certainly free to choose any ideology you wish to adhere to, I would like to ask you, if possible, to please stop spreading these lies once and for all. I've resolved to make this my final visit tonight, as I've said, in the knowledge that I must give up on Adler completely, in your presence and with this feeling in my heart.

PHILOSOPHER: So, was there some event that triggered this?

YOUTH: I will talk this through calmly and in an orderly fashion. First, do you recall that final day three years ago, when I last saw you?

PHILOSOPHER: Of course I do. It was a winter day, with glistening white snow all around.

YOUTH: Yes, it was. The night sky was a beautiful blue, and there was a full moon. That day, under the influence of Adler's ideas, I took a great step forward. I quit my job at the university library and found a teaching position at my old middle school. I thought I'd like to put into practice a kind of education that was based on Adler's ideas, and bring it to as many children as possible.

PHILOSOPHER: Isn't that a wonderful decision?

YOUTH: Sure. I was burning with idealism then. I simply couldn't keep such wonderful, world-changing ideas all to myself. I had to get more people to understand them. But whom? I could arrive at only one conclusion. Adults, who are no longer pure and uncorrupted, aren't the ones who need to know about Adler. It's by bringing them to children, who will build a new generation, that his ideas will continue to evolve. That was the mission I had been assigned. The fire inside me was burning so bright, I might well have burned myself.

PHILOSOPHER: I see. You can speak of this only in the past tense?

YOUTH: That's right; it's totally history now. But please don't misunderstand me. I haven't lost hope in my students. And neither have I lost hope or given up with regard to education itself. It's just that I have lost hope in Adler—which is to say, I have lost hope in you.

PHILOSOPHER: Why is that?

YOUTH: Well, that's something for you to contemplate and ask yourself! Adler's ideas have no use in actual society, and are nothing more than abstract, empty theories. Especially that education principle that states: "One must not praise, and one must not rebuke." And just so you know, I followed it faithfully. I didn't praise, and I didn't rebuke anyone either. I didn't give praise for perfect scores on tests, or for a thorough job cleaning up. I didn't rebuke anyone for forgetting to do their homework, or for being noisy in class. What do you think happened as a result of this?

PHILOSOPHER: . . . Your students became unruly?

YOUTH: Completely. But when I think back on it all now, that was only natural. It was my fault for getting taken in by such cheap quackery.

PHILOSOPHER: So, what did you do about it?

YOUTH: Needless to say, for the students who were misbehaving, I chose the path of stern rebuke. I know you're probably going to make light of that and tell me it was a foolish solution. But look, I'm not a person who busies himself with philosophy and gets lost in daydreams. I am an educator who deals with real, on-the-ground situations, and looks after students' lives and destinies. Because the reality right in front of us is never still—it's moving constantly from moment to moment! You can't just sit back and do nothing!

PHILOSOPHER: How effective is it?

YOUTH: Naturally, if I rebuke them any further, it doesn't do any good. Because they disparage me now—I'm just a softy to them. . . . Honestly, there are even times when I envy the teachers of ages past, when physical punishment was permitted and even standard.

PHILOSOPHER: It's not an easy situation.

YOUTH: True. Just so there isn't any misunderstanding, I should add that I haven't been letting my emotions take over or getting angry. I'm only rebuking, in a rational manner, as a last resort for the purposes of education. I guess you could say I've been prescribing an antibiotic medicine called "reprimand."

PHILOSOPHER: So then you decided to give up on Adler?

YOUTH: Well, I mentioned that just to give you a clear example. Adler's ideas are certainly wonderful. They shake up your value system and make you feel like the cloudy skies over your head are clearing up, like your life has changed. They would seem to be beyond reproach—a universal truth, even. But the fact is that the only place they hold water is right here, in this study! Once you throw open the door and dive into the actual world, Adler's ideas are just too naive. The arguments they put forward are quite impractical, and nothing but empty idealism. You've just been fabricating a world that suits your purposes here in this room and losing yourself in daydreams. You don't know a thing about the real world and the swarming masses of people who live in it!

PHILOSOPHER: I see. . . . And then?

YOUTH: An education in which one neither praises nor rebukes? An education that espouses autonomy and leaves students to fend for themselves? That's nothing other than a renunciation of one's professional duties as an educator. From now on, I am going to face the children in a way that is very different from Adler's. I don't care if it is "right" or not. Because I have no other choice. I will praise, and I will rebuke. And naturally, I will have to mete out harsh punishment as well.

PHILOSOPHER: You're not going to quit working as an educator, are you?

YOUTH: Of course not. I will never give up on the path of being an educator. Because it is the path I have chosen. It is not an occupation, but a way of living.

PHILOSOPHER: It is most reassuring to hear that.

YOUTH: So, you think of this as somebody else's problem? If I'm going to continue as an educator, I have to give up on Adler right here and now! If I don't, I'll be renouncing my responsibilities as an educator and abandoning my students. Well, what is your response to that!?

PHILOSOPHER: First, allow me to make a correction. You used the word "truth" earlier. But I am not presenting Adler as an absolute, immutable truth. One might say that what I am doing is giving a prescription for eyeglass lenses. I believe there are many people whose fields of vision have been broadened as a result of these lenses. On the other hand, there are probably those who say their vision has become even cloudier than before. I do not try to force the lenses of Adler's ideas on them.

YOUTH: Oh, so you run away from them?

PHILOSOPHER: No. Let's look at it this way. No other form of thought is as easy to get wrong and as hard to get right as Adlerian psychology. The majority of those who say, "I know Adler," misunderstand his teachings. They do not possess the courage to approach a true understanding, and they do not try to look directly at the landscape that spreads out beyond this way of thinking.

YOUTH: People misunderstand Adler?

PHILOSOPHER: That's right. If someone comes into contact with Adler's ideas, and is immediately moved very deeply and says, "Life is easier now," that person is grossly misunderstanding Adler. Because when one truly understands what Adler is demanding of us, one is likely to be shocked by its severity.

YOUTH: So, you are saying that I, too, misunderstand Adler?

PHILOSOPHER: Yes, from everything you have been telling me, it would seem so. You are certainly not alone in this, however. There are many Adlerians (practitioners of Adlerian psychology) who misunderstand him at the outset, and then climb the stairway of understanding. It would seem that you haven't actually found the stairway that you should climb yet. I didn't find it right away either, when I was young.

YOUTH: Huh, you had a period when you were lost too?

PHILOSOPHER: Yes, I did.

YOUTH: Then I want you to teach me. Where is this stairway to understanding, or whatever it is? What do you mean by "stairway" anyway? Where did you find it?

PHILOSOPHER: I was fortunate. Because I was a househusband in the midst of raising a young child when I came to know Adler.

YOUTH: What do you mean?

PHILOSOPHER: Through my child, I learned Adler, and together with my child, I was able to practice, and thus deepen my understanding and obtain positive proof of Adler.

YOUTH: So, that's what I'm asking you to tell me! What did you learn? And what is this positive proof you obtained?

PHILOSOPHER: In a word, it was "love."

YOUTH: What did you say?

PHILOSOPHER: . . . You don't really need me to say it again, do you?

YOUTH: Ha-ha, what a laugh! So now it all boils down to love? You're saying that if I want to know the real Adler, I have to know about love?

PHILOSOPHER: You laugh at this word, but you do not yet understand it. The love Adler speaks of is the harshest and most courage-testing task of all.

YOUTH: Oh, please! If you're just going to preach about neighborly love, I don't want to hear it.

PHILOSOPHER: Just now you stated that you have reached a dead end in your role as an educator and, as a consequence, you distrust Adler. Then you are eager to tell me that you are denouncing Adler, and that you don't want me to talk about him anymore either. Why are you so upset? I suppose you felt that Adler's ideas were something like magic. As if you could just wave a wand, and without further ado, all your wishes would be granted.

If that is the case, you should give up on Adler. You should give up the mistaken images of Adler that you have embraced and get to know the real Adler.

YOUTH: No, you're wrong! In the first place, I have never expected Adler to be magical or anything like that. And second, as I think you yourself once said, "Anyone can be happy from this moment onward."

PHILOSOPHER: Yes, I certainly did say that.

YOUTH: But aren't such words a perfect example of magic? You're warning people, "Don't be fooled by that counterfeit money," while pushing other counterfeit money. It's a classic swindler's trick!

PHILOSOPHER: Anyone can be happy from this moment onward. This is an undeniable fact, not magic or anything of the sort. You, and everyone else, can take steps toward happiness. But happiness is not something one can enjoy by staying where one is. One has to keep walking along the path one has embarked on. It is necessary to be clear on this point.

You took the step. You took a big step. Now, however, not only have you lost courage and let your feet come to a halt, you are trying to turn back. Do you know why?

YOUTH: You're saying I don't have patience.

PHILOSOPHER: No. You have not yet made "the biggest choice in life." That's all.

YOUTH: The biggest choice in life! What do I have to choose?

PHILOSOPHER: I said it earlier. You must choose love.

YOUTH: Hah, you expect me to understand that? Please don't try to escape into abstraction!

PHILOSOPHER: I am serious. The issues you are now experiencing all stem from the single notion of "love." The issues you have with education, and also the issue of the kind of life you should lead.

YOUTH: . . . All right. This seems like something worth refuting. Now, before we get into a full-fledged discussion, there is one thing I'd like to say. There is no doubt in my mind that you are a modern-day Socrates. However, it is not his school of thought that I am referring to, but his crime.

PHILOSOPHER: His crime?

YOUTH: Apparently, Socrates was sentenced to death on the suspicion of having tempted and corrupted the youth of the ancient Greek city-state of Athens, right? He subdued his disciples, who were appealing to him to escape from prison, and then drank a poison tea and took leave of this world. It's interesting, isn't it? If you ask me, you who espouse the ideas of Adler here in this ancient capital are guilty of exactly the same crime. In other words, you are tempting and corrupting naive youth with deceitful words!

PHILOSOPHER: You are saying that you were taken in and corrupted by Adler?

YOUTH: That is precisely why I resolved to visit once more before I part ways with you for good. I don't want to create any more victims. Philosophically speaking, I must silence you once and for all.

PHILOSOPHER: Well, then, it's going to be a long night.

YOUTH: But let's settle this tonight, before daybreak. There is no need for me to keep calling on you after this. Will I climb the stairway of understanding? Or will I tear down that stairway of yours and abandon Adler, once and for all? It'll be one or the other; there's no in-between.

PHILOSOPHER: All right. This may be our last dialogue . . . No, it seems we will have to make it our last, no matter what.

PART I
That Bad Person and Poor Me

Little had changed in the philosopher's study since the youth's visit there three years before. A partially written manuscript lay in a loose bundle on the well-used desk. On top of it, perhaps to prevent the papers from being blown about by the wind, lay an old-fashioned fountain pen ornamented with gold inlay. It all felt familiar to the youth; it was almost as if he were in his own room. He noticed several books he owned, including one he had just read a week earlier. Gazing wistfully at the bookshelf, which took up an entire wall, the youth let out a great sigh. *I mustn't get too comfortable here. I've got to keep moving forward.*

Is Adlerian Psychology a Religion?

YOUTH: Before coming to the decision to visit you once more today—that is to say, before making the firm resolution to abandon Adler—I went through a great deal of distress. It troubled me more than you can imagine. That's how attractive Adler's ideas were to me. But the fact is that at the same time that I was attracted to them, I was harboring doubts all along. And those doubts concern the name "Adlerian psychology" itself.

PHILOSOPHER: Hmm. What do you mean?

YOUTH: As the name "Adlerian psychology" indicates, Adler's ideas are regarded as psychology. And as far as I am aware, psychology is essentially a science. When it comes to the opinions put forth by Adler, however, there are aspects that strike me as decidedly unscientific. Of course, as this is an area of study that deals with the psyche, it might not be completely expressible in mathematical form. That I understand perfectly well.

But the problem, you see, is that Adler talks about people in terms of "ideals." He's offering up the same kind of cloying sermons that Christians do when they preach about neighborly love. Which brings me to my first question. Do you think of Adlerian psychology as a science?

PHILOSOPHER: If you are speaking of a strict definition of science, that is to say, a science that has falsifiability, then no, it is not. Adler declared his psychology to be a science, but when he began talking about his concept of "social feeling," many of his colleagues parted ways with him. Their judgment was much like yours: "That sort of thing isn't science."

YOUTH: Right, that's a natural response for anyone who is interested in psychology as a science.

PHILOSOPHER: This is an ongoing area of debate, but Freud's psycho-analysis, Jung's analytical psychology, and Adler's individual psychology all have aspects that come into conflict with such a definition of science in that they do not have falsifiability. This is a fact.

YOUTH: Okay, I see. I've brought my notebook with me today. I'm going to get this down in writing. That strictly speaking . . . it is not science! Now to my next question: Three years ago, you referred to Adler's ideas as "another philosophy," did you not?

PHILOSOPHER: You are correct, I did. I think of Adlerian psychology as a way of thinking that follows in the same vein as Greek philosophy, and that is itself a philosophy. I think the same way about Adler himself. Before regarding him as a psychologist, I see him as a philosopher. He is a philosopher who put his expertise to practical use in clinical settings. This is my perception.

YOUTH: All right. So, here's my main point. I thought hard about Adler's ideas, and I really put them into practice. I wasn't skeptical about them. Rather, it was as if those ideas filled me with a feverish passion, and I believed in them with all my heart. The thing is, whenever I have tried to practice Adler's ideas in an educational setting, the opposition has been overwhelming. I have been opposed not only by the students, but by the other teachers around me. But if you think about it, that makes sense. Because I was presenting an approach to education based on a value sys-tem that is completely different from theirs, and attempting to put it into practice there for the first time. And then I happened to recall a certain group of people, and I superimposed their circumstances onto mine. . . . Do you know who I am talking about?

PHILOSOPHER: Well, no, I don't. Who could it be?

YOUTH: The Catholic missionaries who forayed into the heathen lands during the Age of Discovery.

PHILOSOPHER: Ah.

YOUTH: Africa, Asia, and the Americas. Those Catholic missionaries journeyed into strange lands where the languages, cultures, and even gods were different, and they went around espousing the teachings they believed in. Just like me, who took my post to espouse the ideas of Adler. The missionaries, though they often succeeded in propagating their faith, also experienced oppression and were sometimes even executed by barbaric methods. One would think it common sense that such people would simply be turned away.

But if so, how on earth could these missionaries have succeeded in preaching a new god to the inhabitants of the places they visited, and making them give up their native beliefs? It must have been work of considerable difficulty. Craving to know more, I ran to the library.

PHILOSOPHER: But that's . . .

YOUTH: Wait, I'm not finished. So, while I was poring over various writings on the missionaries of the Age of Discovery, another interesting thought occurred to me: When it comes down to it, isn't Adler's philosophy a religion?

PHILOSOPHER: Interesting . . .

YOUTH: Because it's true, isn't it? The ideals Adler talks about are not science. And to the extent that they are not science, in the end it is just a question of one's level of faith, of either believing or not believing. So, again, it is just about one's feeling. It is true that from our point of view, people who don't know Adler may seem like savage primitives who believe in false gods. And so we feel that we must teach them the real "truth" and save them, as quickly as possible. However, it may be that from their vantage point, we are the ones who are primitive worshippers of wicked gods. Maybe we are the ones who need to be saved. Am I wrong?

PHILOSOPHER: No, you are quite right.

YOUTH: Then tell me: What is the difference between Adler's philosophy and religion?

PHILOSOPHER: The difference between religion and philosophy is an important subject. If you just rule out the existence of God and think about it then, the discussion will be easier to understand.

YOUTH: Ah. What do you mean?

PHILOSOPHER: Religion, philosophy, and science all stem from the same questions: Where do we come from? Where are we? And how should we live? In ancient Greece, there was no division between philosophy and science, and the Latin root of the word "science" is *scientia*, which simply means "knowledge."

YOUTH: Fine, that's how science was back then. But I am asking about philosophy and religion. What is the difference between them?

PHILOSOPHER: It would probably be better to clarify their points of commonality first. Unlike science, which limits itself to objective fact-finding, philosophy and religion also deal with human ideas of truth, good, and beauty. This is an extremely important point.

YOUTH: I know. And philosophy and religion delve into the human psyche. But where, then, are the boundary lines and points of difference between the two? Is it just that single question of whether God exists?

PHILOSOPHER: No. The most important point of difference is the presence or absence of "story." Religion explains the world by means of stories. You could say that gods are the protagonists of the grand stories that religions use to explain the world. By contrast, philosophy rejects stories. It tries to explain the world by means of abstract concepts that have no protagonists.

YOUTH: Philosophy rejects stories?

PHILOSOPHER: Or think of it this way: In our search for truth, we are walking on a long pole that extends into the darkness. Doubting our common sense and engaging in continual self-doubt, we just continue to walk on that pole without any idea of how far it may go. And then, from out of the darkness, one hears a voice inside saying, "Nothing further lies ahead. Here is truth."

YOUTH: Huh . . .

PHILOSOPHER: So, some people stop listening to their internal voice, and stop walking. They jump down from the pole. Do they find truth there? I don't know. Maybe they do, maybe they don't. But stopping in one's steps and jumping off the pole midway is what I call "religion." With philosophy, one keeps walking without end. It doesn't matter if there are gods or not.

YOUTH: Then, this walking-without-end philosophy doesn't have any answers?

PHILOSOPHER: In the original Greek, *philosophia* has the meaning "love of wisdom." In other words, philosophy is "the study of the love of wisdom," and philosophers are "lovers of wisdom." Conversely, one could say that if a person were to become a complete "wise man" who knows all there is to know, that person would no longer be a lover of wisdom (philosopher). In the words of Kant, the giant of modern philosophy, "We cannot learn philosophy. We can only learn to philosophize."

YOUTH: To *philosophize?*

PHILOSOPHER: That's right. Philosophy is more of a living attitude than a field of study. Religion may convey "all" under the name of God. It may convey an all-knowing, almighty God and the teachings handed down by that God. This is a way of thinking that conflicts fundamentally with philosophy.

And someone who purports to know everything, who has stopped in their path of knowing and thinking, regardless of their belief in the existence or nonexistence of God, or even the presence or absence of their faith, is venturing into religion. That is my view on the matter.

YOUTH: In other words, you still "don't know" the answers?

PHILOSOPHER: No, I do not. The instant we feel that we "know" about the object, we want to seek beyond it. I will always think about myself, other people, and the world. Therefore, I will "not know" without end.

YOUTH: Heh-heh. That answer is philosophical too.

PHILOSOPHER: Socrates, in his dialogues with the self-described wise men known as the Sophists, arrived at the following conclusion: "I (Socrates) know that my knowledge is not complete. I know my own ignorance. The Sophists, on the other hand, those would-be wise men, intend to understand 'everything' and know nothing of their own ignorance. In this respect—my knowledge of my own ignorance—I am more of a wise man than they are." This is the context of Socrates's famous statement, "I know that I know nothing."

YOUTH: Then what can you, who have no answers and are ignorant, impart to me?

PHILOSOPHER: I will not impart. Let's think and walk together.

YOUTH: Ah, to the end of the pole? Without jumping off?

PHILOSOPHER: That's right. Keep inquiring and keep walking, without limit.

YOUTH: You're so confident, even though you say that sophistry won't hold water. All right. I'm going to shake you down off that pole!

The Objective of Education
Is Self-Reliance

PHILOSOPHER: Well, where should we begin?

YOUTH: The problem that requires my urgent attention right now is education. So I'll expose Adler's contradictions with a focus on that. Because there are all manner of aspects of Adler's ideas that, at their core, are incompatible with education.

PHILOSOPHER: I see. That sounds interesting.

YOUTH: In Adlerian psychology, there is a way of thinking called "separation of tasks," right? All sorts of things and events in life are regarded from the viewpoint of "Whose task is this?" and divided into "one's own tasks" and "other people's tasks." Say, for example, that my boss doesn't like me. Naturally, it doesn't feel good. It would be normal to make some effort to be liked by him and seek his approval somehow.

But Adler considers that to be wrong. What kind of judgment do other people (in this case, my boss) pass on my speech and conduct, and on me as a person? That is the boss's task (other people's tasks) and is not something I can control. No matter how much I try to be liked by him, my boss might just continue to dislike me.

On this point, Adler says, "You are not living to satisfy other people's expectations." And further, "Other people are not living to satisfy your expectations." Don't be afraid of who might be watching; don't pay attention to other people's judgment; and don't seek recognition from others.

Just choose the path that is best for you, and that you believe in. Furthermore, you must not intervene in other people's tasks, and you must not allow others to intervene in your tasks either. To those who are new to Adlerian psychology, this is a concept that has a great impact.

PHILOSOPHER: True. Being able to carry out the separation of tasks dramatically reduces one's interpersonal relationship problems.

YOUTH: You also said this: There is an easy way to determine who has which task. I should think, "Who ultimately is going to receive the end result brought about by that choice?" I'm not getting it wrong, am I?

PHILOSOPHER: No, you are not.

YOUTH: The example you used then was that of studying for a child—a child who does not study. His parents are anxious about his future, and yell at him to hit the books. But who is going to receive the end result brought about by not studying—that is to say, that he won't be able to get into the desired school, or that it will be more difficult for him to find a job? No matter how you look at it, it's the child himself, not the parents. In other words, studying is the child's task, and is not an issue in which the parents should intervene. Am I doing okay so far?

PHILOSOPHER: You are.

YOUTH: Now, this is where a major doubt arises. Studying is the child's task. One must not intervene in the child's tasks. But if so, then what is this thing we call "education"? What is this occupation we are engaging in as educators? Because if one abides by your line of reasoning, we educators who push children to study are just a gang of trespassers who intrude on their tasks! Now, how can you answer that?

PHILOSOPHER: Okay, well, this is a question that comes up on occasion when I discuss Adler with educators. Studying is certainly the child's task. No one is permitted to intervene there, not even the parents. If the separation of tasks Adler speaks of is interpreted in a one-dimensional way, all forms of education become interventions into other people's tasks, and thus, reprehensible conduct. In Adler's time, however, there was no psychologist more concerned with education. To Adler, education was not simply a core task—it was also the greatest hope.

YOUTH: Hmm. Can you be more concrete?

PHILOSOPHER: For example, in Adlerian psychology, counseling is thought of not as "treatment," but as a place for "reeducation."

YOUTH: Reeducation?

PHILOSOPHER: That's right. Counseling and childhood education are essentially the same. The counselor is an educator, and the educator is a counselor. It is fine to think of it in this way.

YOUTH: Ha-ha, I didn't know that! I had no idea I was a counselor! What on earth is that supposed to mean?

PHILOSOPHER: This is an important point. Let's straighten things out as we continue the discussion. First, what is the intended objective of education, both at home and at school? What is your view on this?

YOUTH: It's not something I can convey in just a few words. The cultivation of knowledge through scholarship, the attainment of social skills, the development of human beings who respect justice, and who are sound in mind and body . . .

PHILOSOPHER: Yes. All these are important, but let's look at the bigger picture. What does one want children to become as a result of one's providing them with an education?

YOUTH: One wants them to become independent adults?

PHILOSOPHER: Right. The objective of education, in a word, is self-reliance.

YOUTH: Self-reliance . . . Well, I guess you could put it that way.

PHILOSOPHER: In Adlerian psychology, all people are regarded as beings who live their lives with the desire to escape from their helpless conditions and improve themselves. That is to say, in the "pursuit of superiority." The toddling baby learns how to stand on two legs, acquires language, and becomes able to communicate with the people around him. In other words, what all people are seeking is freedom from their helpless and unfree conditions, and self-reliance. These are fundamental desires.

YOUTH: So, education is what promotes this self-reliance?

PHILOSOPHER: Exactly. And for children to both grow physically and become socially self-reliant, there are all manner of things that they need to know. They need the social skills and the sense of justice you mentioned, and they probably need knowledge and other things too. And, of course, the things they do not know must be taught to them by other people who do. The people around them must give their assistance. Education is not intervention, but assistance toward self-reliance.

YOUTH: It sounds to me like you're desperately trying to rephrase things!

PHILOSOPHER: For example, how would it be if one were thrown into society without knowing any traffic rules, without knowing the meaning of red lights and green lights? Or if one had no car-driving skills, and found oneself behind the wheel? Naturally, there are rules to be learned here, and skills to be attained. This is an issue of life or death and, moreover, of putting other people's lives in danger as well. One could also put it the other way around and say that if there were no other people left on earth and you were the only person alive, there would not be anything you would have to know, and education would not be necessary, either. You would not have any need for knowledge.

YOUTH: It's because of other people and society that there is knowledge that should be studied?

PHILOSOPHER: Yes! "Knowledge" here refers not only to scholarly studies but includes the knowledge that people need to live happily. In short, how one should live within a community. How one should interact with others. How one can locate one's proper place in that community. To know "me" and to know "you." To know the true nature of a person, and to understand the way in which a person ought to live. Adler referred to such knowledge as "human knowledge."

YOUTH: Human knowledge? I've never heard that term before.

PHILOSOPHER: I don't suppose you would have. This human knowledge is not the kind of knowledge that is gained from books—it is something that can only be learned by actually being engaged in relationships with other people. In that sense, one could say that the school, in which one is surrounded by large numbers of other people, is a more meaningful place of education than the home.

YOUTH: So, you're saying that the key to education is this thing you call "human knowledge"?

PHILOSOPHER: That's right. It's the same with counseling. The counselor assists the client in gaining self-reliance. And they think together about the human knowledge that is necessary for self-reliance. Do you recall the objectives put forth by Adlerian psychology that we were discussing last time? The behavioral objectives and the psychological objectives?

YOUTH: Yes, I remember them. There are two objectives for behavior:

1. To be self-reliant
2. To live in harmony with society

And there are two objectives for the psychology that supports these behaviors:

1. The consciousness that *I have the ability*
2. The consciousness that *people are my comrades*

So, briefly put, you are saying that these four things are valuable, not only in counseling, but in an actual educational setting?

PHILOSOPHER: And they are no less valuable to us adults, with our general feelings of how hard life is. Because there are so many adults suffering in social settings who are unable to attain these objectives.

If one has left behind the objective of self-reliance, whether in education, counseling, or job coaching, very quickly one will end up forcing things.

We must be aware of the roles we are playing—whether we are letting education fall into a kind of trap of compulsory intervention, or limiting ourselves to a self-reliance–stimulating assistance. It is something that depends on the approach of the person who is doing the educating, counseling, or coaching.

YOUTH: It would certainly seem so. I get it, and I agree with these lofty ideals; I really do. But, look, you've already tried that trick on me, and it won't work anymore! Whatever we talk about, it always turns into abstract idealism in the end. It just turns into me listening to these big, feel-good words of yours, and thinking I understand.

But my issues aren't abstract ones—they're actually quite concrete. Instead of all these empty theories, let's hear a grounded, practical theory.

Concretely, what sort of step can I take as an educator? That most important, concrete first step—you've been dodging that point all along, haven't you? What you're talking about is such a faraway thing. It's as if you're always going on about some landscape far in the distance and trying not to look at the mud at your feet!

Three years earlier, the youth had been filled with astonishment and doubt on hearing the ideas of Adler conveyed by the philosopher, and he had expressed his opposition to them with the fiercest emotion. It was different this time, though. He had a sufficient understanding now of the framework of Adlerian psychology, and moreover, he had gained actual experience in society. One might even say that, in the sense that he had on-the-job experience, *he* was the one who had learned more. This time, the youth had a clear plan. *Focus not on the abstract, but on the concrete. Not on theory, but on actual practice. And not on ideals, but on reality. That is what I want to know, and also where Adler's weaknesses lie.*

Respect Is Seeing People as They Are

PHILOSOPHER: Concretely, then, where should we begin? When education, coaching, and assistance adopt self-reliance as their objective, where is the point of entry? To be sure, this may be an area of concern. But there are clear guidelines here.

YOUTH: I'm all ears.

PHILOSOPHER: There is only one answer: respect.

YOUTH: Respect?

PHILOSOPHER: Yes. No other point of entry is possible in education.

YOUTH: Another surprising answer! So, in other words, what you're saying is: respect your parents, respect your teachers, and respect your boss?

PHILOSOPHER: No. First of all, for example, in a class, *you* must have respect for the children. Everything starts from there.

YOUTH: *I* do? For these kids who can't be quiet and listen to someone for even five minutes?

PHILOSOPHER: Yes. It could be a relationship between parent and child, or within a company organization, but it doesn't matter—in any kind of interpersonal relationship, it is the same. Initially, the parent respects the child, and the boss respects his subordinates. The roles are such that the person standing on the "teaching side" has respect for the person standing on the "learning side." Without respect, no good interpersonal relationships can come about, and without good relations, one's words will not reach anyone.

YOUTH: You're saying I should respect each and every problem child?

PHILOSOPHER: Yes. Because at the root of it is "respect for people." One's respect is not limited to specific others, but extends to other people of all kinds, from family and friends, to unknown passersby, and even to people in other countries whom one will never meet as long as one lives.

YOUTH: Ah, another lecture on morality! Or else it's religion. Well, I've got to say, you're giving me a good opening. It's true that morality is included in the curriculum in school education, that it has such importance. And I concede that there are many people who believe in those values.

But consider this. Why is it even necessary to talk sense into children about morality? It's because children are immoral beings by nature, as are all humans! Heck, what is "respect for people" anyway? Moreover, within both of us, in the very depths of our souls, there drifts the repulsively putrid stink of immorality!

You preach on what is moral to immoral people. I am seeking morality. This truly is intervention, nothing less than force. The things you say are full of contradictions. I'll say it again: Your idealism will have no effect at all in an actual situation. And besides, how can you expect me to respect these problem children?

PHILOSOPHER: Then I will say it again too: I am not preaching morality. But the other point is that, especially with people like you, I have to help you to understand and to actually practice respect.

YOUTH: Well, enough of that already! I don't want to hear empty theories that reek of religion. I'm asking you for concrete examples that are practicable tomorrow.

PHILOSOPHER: What is respect? Here is one definition: "Respect denotes the ability to see a person as [they are]; to be aware of [their] unique individuality." These are the words of the social psychologist Erich Fromm, who moved from Germany to America to escape Nazi persecution around the same time as Adler.

YOUTH: The ability to be aware of their unique individuality?

PHILOSOPHER: Yes. One sees "that person," who is irreplaceable and utterly unique in the world, just as they are. Moreover, Fromm adds, "Respect means the concern that the other person should grow and unfold as [they are]."

YOUTH: I don't understand.

PHILOSOPHER: Not trying to change or manipulate the other person who is right there in front of you. Accepting that person as they are without setting any conditions. There is no greater respect than this. Then, on being accepted by another person "as one is," one is likely to gain a great courage. And respect may also be regarded as the starting point of encouragement.

YOUTH: No way! That is not the respect that I know. Respect is a kind of emotion akin to yearning, a sort of imploring that one can rise to the occasion!

PHILOSOPHER: No. That is not respect, but fear, subordination, and faith. It is a state in which one fears power and authority, and worships false images without seeing anything of the other person.

The Latin *Respicio*, which is the root of "respect," has the connotation of "seeing." First of all, one sees the person as they are. You have not seen anything yet, and neither have you tried to see. Place value on the person "being that person" without pushing your own value system on them. And further, assist in their growth or unfolding. That is precisely what respect is. In the attitude of trying to manipulate or correct another person, there is no respect whatsoever.

YOUTH: So, if I accept them as they are, will these problem children change?

PHILOSOPHER: That is not something you can control. Maybe they will change, and maybe they will not. But as a result of your respect, each of the students will accept themselves for being who they are, and regain the courage to be self-reliant. There is no doubting this. Whether they use their regained courage is up to each student.

YOUTH: So that's the separation of tasks?

PHILOSOPHER: That's right. You can lead them to water, but you can't make them drink. No matter how gifted you are as an educator, there is no guarantee that they will change. But it is precisely because there is no such guarantee that one has unconditional respect. First *you* have to start. Without setting any conditions whatsoever, and regardless of what the anticipated results might be, it is you who take the first step.

YOUTH: But nothing will change that way.

PHILOSOPHER: In this world, no matter how powerful one is, there are two things that cannot be forced.

YOUTH: What are they?

PHILOSOPHER: Respect and love. For example, let's say the person at the top of a company organization is an authoritarian despot. The employees will follow his orders, certainly. And they will probably display obedient behavior. But that is submission based on fear, without an iota of respect. He can shout "respect me!," but none of them will comply. In their hearts, they will just grow more and more distant from him.

YOUTH: Yes, I'm sure they will.

PHILOSOPHER: On top of that, if no mutual respect exists, then there is no "relationship" as human beings either. An organization like that is just assembling groups of humans to function as its nuts and bolts and gears. It can carry out machinelike labor, but no one else can do the human "work."

YOUTH: Okay, enough roundabout talk already! So, basically what you're saying is that I'm not respected by my students, and that's why the classroom gets out of control?

PHILOSOPHER: If there is fear even for a short time, it is unlikely for there to be any respect. It's only natural that the class will get out of control. You just stood by idly as it developed, and now you resort to authoritarian measures. You use power and fear to try to make them do your bidding. Maybe you can expect that to be effective for a while. Maybe you'll feel relieved that they really seem to be listening to you now. However . . .

YOUTH: They're not hearing a single word that comes out of my mouth.

PHILOSOPHER: That's right. The children are not obeying "you," they are only submitting to authority. They do not entertain the slightest thought of understanding "you." They just cover their ears and shut their eyes and wait for the storm of your rage to pass.

YOUTH: Heh-heh, you've really hit the nail on the head.

PHILOSOPHER: You fall into this vicious cycle because you fail to take the initial step of respecting the students yourself, of respecting them unconditionally.

YOUTH: So, because I failed to take that step, there is nothing I can do that will get through to them?

PHILOSOPHER: That's right. You have been shouting to an empty room. There's no way they can hear you.

YOUTH: Okay, fine, I understand that. There are still so many points I need to refute, but I'll accept this for the time being. Now, supposing that your approach is the right one—that relationships are built on the basis of respect. How, then, does one show respect? You're not telling me to put on a pleasant smile and say, "Hey, I respect you," are you?

PHILOSOPHER: Respect is not something that comes about with words. And whenever an adult tries to cozy up to them in such a way, the children quickly detect the lie or calculation. The moment they think, "This person is lying," respect isn't possible anymore.

YOUTH: Okay, okay. You've hit the nail on the head again. But what are you suggesting I should do? Because there's actually a major contradiction in the way you're talking about respect right now.

PHILOSOPHER: Oh? What contradiction is that?

Start from respect, the philosopher was saying. And that respect is not only the foundation on which education is built, but it is also the base of all interpersonal relationships. Certainly, one doesn't pay much attention to the words of people one doesn't respect. There were aspects of the philosopher's arguments that the youth could agree with. But the argument that one had to respect all other people—that even the problem children in his classroom, and the villains at large in society, were all worthy of respect—that was something he opposed vehemently. *He's dug his own grave. He's made a contradiction that can't be overlooked. So, this is something I must do, after all. I have to metaphorically seal this Socrates in his cave.* The youth pondered this for a moment, and then continued at full speed.

Have Concern for Other People's Concerns

YOUTH: Don't you see? Earlier, you said, "Respect can never be forced." Sure, that is probably the case. That I can agree with wholeheartedly. But then, in the same breath, you tell me to "respect the students." Ha-ha, isn't it funny? You're trying to force me to do something that apparently can't be forced! If you don't call that a contradiction, then what is?

PHILOSOPHER: It is true that if you pick out just those statements on their own, they might sound contradictory. But look at it this way. Respect is a ball that comes back to you only from the person to whom you pass it. It's just like throwing a ball at a wall. If you throw it, it might come back to you. But nothing is going to happen if you just face the wall and shout, "Give me the ball."

YOUTH: No way, I'm not going to let you get away with half-baked metaphors. Give me a proper answer. If I'm the one throwing that ball of respect, where does it come from? The ball doesn't just come out of nowhere!

PHILOSOPHER: All right. This is an important point about understanding and practicing Adlerian psychology. Do you recall the term "social feeling"?

YOUTH: Of course. Though I wouldn't say I understand it completely.

PHILOSOPHER: Yes, it's a rather difficult concept. Let's consider it more thoroughly another time. For the time being, though, I would like you to recall Adler's use of the term "social interest" when translating the original German term for "social feeling" into English. This social interest means our "concern for society," or more simply, our concern for the other people who make up society.

YOUTH: So, it's different in the original German?

PHILOSOPHER: Yes. The German term is *Gemeinschaftsgefühl*, which combines *Gemeinschaft*, meaning "social relations" or "community," with *Gefühl* ("sense" or "feeling"), which I translate as "social feeling." If one were to give it an English translation that is more faithful to the original German, one might call it "community feeling" or "community sense."

YOUTH: Well, I am not particularly interested in such academic talk, but what about it?

PHILOSOPHER: Think about it for a moment. Why, when Adler introduced this idea to the English-speaking world, did he choose "social interest" instead of "social feeling," which is closer to the German? There is an important hidden motive here.

Do you remember how I said that when Adler first put forward the concept of social feeling during his Vienna period, many of his colleagues parted ways with him? That he was opposed and ostracized by people who said that such stuff wasn't science, and that he had introduced the problem of "value" into the otherwise scientific field of psychology?

YOUTH: Yes, I remember that.

PHILOSOPHER: It is likely that through this experience, Adler understood sufficiently well the difficulty of getting people to understand "social feeling." So, when it came time to introduce the concept to the English-speaking world, he replaced "social feeling" with behavioral guidelines that were based on actual practice. He replaced the abstract idea with something concrete. And these concrete behavioral guidelines may be summarized with the words "concern for others."

YOUTH: Behavioral guidelines?

PHILOSOPHER: Yes. To get away from one's attachment to oneself, and to have concern for other people. If one progresses in accordance with these guidelines, one arrives at social feeling as a matter of course.

YOUTH: I haven't the faintest idea what you're talking about now! Your argument has already become abstract again. The very idea of there being "behavioral guidelines" for having concern for other people . . . Speaking concretely, what should one do, and how?

PHILOSOPHER: Here, it would do well to recall that quote from Erich Fromm: "Respect means the concern that the other person should grow and unfold as [they are]." Without negating anything, or forcing anything, one accepts and values the person as they are. In other words, one protects, and one has concern for, another person's dignity. Do you see where that concrete first step lies?

YOUTH: No. Where?

PHILOSOPHER: This is a quite logical conclusion. It lies in having concern for other people's concerns.

YOUTH: Other people's concerns?

PHILOSOPHER: For example, the children enjoy playing in a way that is completely beyond your understanding. They get absorbed with utterly inane, childish toys. Sometimes they read books that are offensive to public order and morals and indulge in video games. You know what I am referring to, yes?

YOUTH: Sure. I see such things almost every day.

PHILOSOPHER: There are many parents and educators who disapprove and try to give them things that are more "useful" or "worthwhile." They advise against such activities, confiscate the books and toys, and allow the children only what has been determined to have value.

The parent does this "for the child's sake," of course. Even so, one must regard this as an act that is completely lacking in respect, and that only increases the parent's distance from the child. Because it is negating the child's natural concerns.

YOUTH: Okay, so I should recommend vulgar pastimes?

PHILOSOPHER: One does not recommend anything from where one stands. One only has concern for the children's concerns. Try to understand just how vulgar their pastimes are from your point of view, and what they really are, first of all. Try them yourself, and even play together on occasion. Rather than simply playing with them, enjoy the activity yourself. If you do, the children may at last have the real feeling that they are being recognized; that they are not being treated as children; that they are being given respect as individual human beings.

YOUTH: But that's . . .

PHILOSOPHER: Nor is this limited to children. It is the concrete first step of the respect that is sought in all interpersonal relationships. Whether in interpersonal relationships at one's workplace, in relationships between lovers, in international relationships, or what have you, we need to have more concern for other people's concerns.

YOUTH: That's impossible! Maybe you aren't aware of this, but those children's concerns include things that are just too depraved! Things that are indecent, grotesque, and offensive. Isn't it our role as adults to show them the right path?

PHILOSOPHER: No, it is not. Regarding social feeling, Adler liked to use the following expression. What we need is "seeing with the eyes of another, listening with the ears of another, and feeling with the heart of another."

YOUTH: Huh?

PHILOSOPHER: Right now, you are trying to see with your own eyes, listen with your own ears, and feel with your own heart. That is why you refer to the children's concerns using such words as "depraved" and "offensive." The children do not think of them as depraved. Then what are they seeing? One starts by understanding that first.

YOUTH: No, I can't! That's just beyond me.

PHILOSOPHER: Why?

If We Had "the Same Kind
of Heart and Life"

YOUTH: You may have forgotten it, but I remember it well. Three years ago, you made an assertion that went something like this: None of us live in an objective world, but instead in a subjective world that we ourselves have given meaning to. The issue that we must focus on is not "how the world is," but "how we are" and "how we see the world." And also, we cannot escape our own subjectivity.

PHILOSOPHER: Yes, that's right.

YOUTH: Then tell me this: How is it possible that we who cannot escape subjectivity could have "the eyes of another," "the ears of another," or even "the heart of another"? If only you would stop playing around with words!

PHILOSOPHER: This is a crucial point. It is true that one cannot escape subjectivity. And one cannot become another person, of course. However, one can imagine what appears in other people's eyes, and one can imagine the sounds their ears hear.

Adler proposes the following: First of all, think, *What if I had the same kind of heart and life as this person?* If one does that, one should be able to understand that *I would probably be faced with the same sort of task as this person.* And from that point, one should be able to imagine further, that *I would probably deal with it in the same sort of way.*

YOUTH: The same kind of heart and life?

PHILOSOPHER: Say, for example, that there is a student who never even tries to study. Questioning the student by saying, "Why don't you study?" is an attitude completely lacking in respect. Instead, start by thinking, *What if I had the same heart as him? What if I had the same life as him?* In other words, one thinks what it would be like if one were the same age as the student, lived in the same household, and had the same friends and the same interests and concerns. If one does so, one should then be able to imagine what sort of attitude "that self" would adopt upon being faced with the task of one's studies, or why "that self" would refuse to study. Do you know what this sort of attitude is called?

YOUTH: Imagination?

PHILOSOPHER: No. This is what we call "empathy."

YOUTH: Empathy? That's what you call thinking about what it would be like to have the same kind of heart and life as another person?

PHILOSOPHER: Yes. What is generally thought of as empathy—that is to say, agreeing with another person's opinion and sharing their feelings—is actually sympathy. Empathy is a skill, an attitude, that one has when walking side by side with another.

YOUTH: A skill! Empathy is a skill?

PHILOSOPHER: That's right. And since it is a skill, it is something that you too can attain.

YOUTH: Oh, well, isn't this interesting? Okay, then I want you to explain it as a skill. How can one know the other person's "heart and life" or whatever you call it, anyway? By counseling each person, one by one? Hah, there's no way you could learn such things!

PHILOSOPHER: That's exactly why one has concern for other people's concerns. One must not just observe from a distance. One must dive in oneself. Right now, you are standing in a high place and, without ever diving in, making remarks like, "There's no way to do this," or "There's such a barrier." There is no respect in that approach, and no empathy either.

YOUTH: No way—you're wrong! That's totally wrong!

PHILOSOPHER: What is wrong about it?

Courage Is Contagious, and Respect Is Contagious Too

YOUTH: Sure, if I were to run around chasing after a ball together with my students, they might like me more. It might make a good impression on them and give them a feeling of closeness. But if I come down to the level of being a "friend" to those kids, educating them will be even harder.

It's sad to say, but those children are no angels. They're little demons who, the second I go the slightest bit easy on them, will take advantage of me and get too big for their britches, and then they'll be totally out of control. You're living in a fantasy world inhabited by angels who don't really exist!

PHILOSOPHER: I raised two children myself. And there are many young people who come to this study for counseling who weren't able to adapt to school education. As you say, children are not angels. They are human beings.

However, precisely because they are human beings, one must pay them the highest level of respect. One does not look down at them, and neither does one look up at them or flatter them. One interacts with them as equals and has empathy for their interests and concerns.

YOUTH: I'm sorry, but that reason for paying them respect doesn't sit right with me. Basically, what you mean by respecting them is just stroking their egos, right? That's exactly the sort of behavior that is degrading to children.

PHILOSOPHER: It seems that you understand only half of what I have been talking about. I am not seeking one-sided respect from you. Rather, I want you to teach respect to your students.

YOUTH: To teach them respect?

PHILOSOPHER: That's right. By practicing it yourself, you will show them what it means to have respect. Teach them how to build the kind of respect that is the cornerstone of all interpersonal relationships, and show them what a respect-based relationship can be. As Adler tells us, "Cowardice is contagious. And courage is contagious too." Naturally, respect also becomes contagious.

YOUTH: Courage and respect are contagious!

PHILOSOPHER: Yes. And it begins with you. Even if there is no one who understands or supports you, first you must carry the torch, and show courage and respect. Your torch will brighten only a few yards around you at most. It might seem like you're on a lonesome night road, all on your own. But the light you carry will reach the eyes of someone hundreds of yards away. They will know then that a person, a light, a path is there, if they go to it. Eventually, dozens and then hundreds of lights will gather around you. Lights radiated by dozens and hundreds of your comrades.

YOUTH: What kind of allegory is that? I'm guessing what you're saying is this: the role that we educators are assigned is to respect the children, show them what respect is, and get them to learn respect. Have I got that right?

PHILOSOPHER: Yes. That is where the first step lies, not only in education, but in all manner of interpersonal relationships.

YOUTH: No way—I don't care how many children you've raised or how many people you've given counseling to here. You're a philosopher who's been shut up in his study. You don't know a thing about society or school in the real, modern-day world!

Look, what people want from school education, and what people want in a capitalist society, is not this stuff about personal character, or some obscure "human knowledge," or whatever. Parents and guardians and society are looking for real results. And if you're talking about the place where education happens, then the thing we're looking for is scholastic improvement.

PHILOSOPHER: Yes, I suppose so.

YOUTH: No matter how much their students might like them, educators who don't raise scholastic achievement will be branded as unfit to be teachers. It sounds just like a money-losing venture made up of a group of friends. On the other hand, an educator who contributes to scholastic improvement with all their students completely under their thumb will be showered with acclaim.

But we haven't even gotten to the main issue yet. Even the students who have been thoroughly and continuously rebuked will later say, "Thank you very much for coaching me so rigorously back then," and convey their gratitude. They recognize that it is because of the strict treatment that they kept up their studies, and that my strictness was really a "loving whip," as it were, and they go so far as to thank me. How can you explain this reality?

PHILOSOPHER: Naturally, I would say that such a story is quite possible. Actually, one might even regard it as a perfect model case for relearning the theories of Adlerian psychology.

YOUTH: Oh, so you are saying it is explainable?

PHILOSOPHER: Keeping in mind the discussion we engaged in three years ago, let us enter into a slightly deeper place within Adlerian psychology. There are many realizations to be had therein.

"Social feeling"—a key concept of Adlerian psychology, and the most difficult one to grasp. The philosopher spoke of it as "seeing with the eyes of another, listening with the ears of another, and feeling with the heart of another." And said that it requires empathy, which is to have concern for other people's concerns. It made sense, in theory. But was it the educator's job to become someone who truly understands children? Wasn't that just the philosopher playing with language again? The youth glared pointedly at this philosopher who could bring up such words as "relearning" with little to no explanation.

The Real Reason Why
One "Can't Change"

YOUTH: Let's hear it. What am I supposed to relearn about Adler?

PHILOSOPHER: When you look at your speech and conduct, and at other people's speech and conduct, think about the goals that are hidden in them. This is a basic way of thinking in Adlerian psychology.

YOUTH: I know. It's teleology, right?

PHILOSOPHER: Would you give a simple explanation of it?

YOUTH: I will try. Regardless of what may have occurred in the past, nothing is determined by it. It does not matter if there are past traumas either. Because human beings are not driven by past "causes" but live according to present "goals." Suppose, for example, a person says, "My home environment was bad, and that's why I have a dark personality." This is a life-lie. The truth is that the person has the goal of "I don't want to get hurt by getting involved with other people," and in order to real-ize that goal, they choose a "dark personality" that doesn't get involved with anyone. Then, as an excuse for having chosen such a personality themselves, they bring up their past home environment. It's something like that, right?

PHILOSOPHER: Yes. Please continue.

YOUTH: In other words, we are not creatures who are determined by past events. Rather, we determine our own lives according to *the meaning we give* to those events.

PHILOSOPHER: That's right.

YOUTH: And then you said something like this: No matter what has occurred in your life until now, it has no bearing at all on how you live your life from now on. And that you, living "here and now," are the one who decides your own life. So, did I get anything wrong?

PHILOSOPHER: Thank you. No, you did not get anything wrong. We humans are not so fragile as to simply be at the mercy of past traumas. Adler's ideas are based on a strong belief in human dignity and the potential that *human beings can determine themselves at any time.*

YOUTH: Yes, I know that. It's just that I cannot get past the strength of the "causes." It's hard to speak of everything as just being "goals." Because, for example, even if I had the goal of "not wanting to be involved with other people," there would have to be causes somewhere that gave rise to those goals. To me, that teleology is not an almighty truth, even if it is a revolutionary viewpoint.

PHILOSOPHER: That is fine. Something might change through this dialogue here tonight, and something might not. That is for you to decide, and I will not force you. Now, please hear this as one way of thinking.

We are beings who are capable of determining ourselves at any time. We can choose new selves. Yet it is not so easy to change oneself. One might have a strong wish to change but be unable to. Why is this? Can you tell me your opinion?

YOUTH: Because one doesn't really want to change?

PHILOSOPHER: That about sums it up. And this is also connected to the question "What is change?" If we go out on a limb and take it to an extreme, carrying out change is "death itself."

YOUTH: Death itself?

PHILOSOPHER: Suppose, for example, that you are in distress over your life right now. Let's say that you are wishing you could change yourself. But changing yourself means giving up on, denying, and never again showing the face of "yourself until now," as if you were sending it to its grave, in effect. Because once you have done that, you will be reborn as your "new self" at last.

Now, regardless of how dissatisfied you may be with your current situation, can you choose "death"? Can you throw yourself into the bottomless darkness? This is not such an easy thing to accomplish.

That is why people do not try to change, and why they want to feel "okay with things as they are," no matter how tough life gets. And they end up living in search of "okay as I am" ingredients in order to affirm their current situation.

YOUTH: Hmm.

PHILOSOPHER: So, when a person is actively trying to affirm "myself now," what kind of tone do you think it will give to that person's past?

YOUTH: Umm, in other words . . .

PHILOSOPHER: There is only one answer. In short, it would be to sum up their past by saying, "I've been through a lot, but I'm fine with it."

YOUTH: In order to affirm "now," one also affirms "the past" that was unhappy.

PHILOSOPHER: Yes. The people you mentioned earlier, who convey their gratitude by saying, "Thank you very much for rebuking me so harshly back then"—they are all actively trying to affirm "myself now." As a result, their entire past turns into good memories. They are not going to recognize their authoritarian education with only those words of gratitude they conveyed to you.

YOUTH: Since they want to feel, "I'm fine with this," their past turns into good memories. It's intriguing. As an academic psychology, it is a very interesting line of inquiry. However, I cannot agree with your interpretations. Why, you ask? Because I am proof. I do not fit in this model at all! To this day, I am resentful of all the strict and unreasonable teachers I had in my years in middle school and high school, and right or wrong, I am not grateful to them. There is no way that my school life, which was like prison time to me, could ever turn into good memories.

PHILOSOPHER: That must be because you are not satisfied with "myself now."

YOUTH: What did you say?

PHILOSOPHER: To put it more bluntly, in order to justify a "myself now" that is far from ideal, you are painting your entire past the same shade of gray. You are trying to think of it as "that school's fault" or "because of that teacher." And then you are trying to live in possibility: "If it had been the ideal school and I'd met the ideal teacher, I never would have ended up this way."

YOUTH: That's ... that's beyond rude! What grounds do you have to make such assumptions?

46

PHILOSOPHER: Can you really say for sure that I am making assumptions? Because the question is not whether something happened in the past, but what meaning "myself now" gives to that past.

YOUTH: Retract that! What do you know about me?

PHILOSOPHER: Look, in our world, "the past" in the real sense of the word does not exist. It is just painted in an endless array of colors of "now," each with its own interpretations.

YOUTH: In this world, the past does not exist?

PHILOSOPHER: That's right. The past is not something that cannot be regained. Rather, it simply and purely *does not exist*. Until one takes it that far, one cannot get any closer to the essence of teleology.

YOUTH: Argh, this is exasperating! You make assumptions, and then say things like "the past does not exist"? You're tossing out hole-filled falsehoods left and right, and then you're trying to blow smoke. I'm going to have fun dredging the muck out of all those holes and throwing it right back at you!

Your Now Decides the Past

PHILOSOPHER: It is true that this argument is difficult to accept. But if you calmly lay out all the facts, I am sure you will agree. Because there is no other path here.

YOUTH: Well, it seems to me that the heat of your passion for these ideas has burned a hole in your head. If you say the past doesn't exist, then how do you explain history? Maybe your beloved Socrates and Plato didn't exist? Look, that's what you're implying, so you're going to be ridiculed as unscientific.

PHILOSOPHER: History is a grand story that is continually manipulated by the powers that be of the time. It is always manipulated with great skill on the basis of the logic of the powerful to say, "It is I who am just." All chronologies and history books are apocrypha compiled for the purpose of proving the legitimacy of those currently in power.

In history, it is always the "now" that is the most correct, and whenever one authority is overthrown, a new ruler will rewrite the past again. But they will do so only for the purpose of explaining their own legitimacy. So "the past," in the most basic sense of the word, does not exist.

YOUTH: But . . . !!

PHILOSOPHER: For example, suppose an armed group of a certain country is planning a coup d'état. If they are suppressed and the attempt

48

ends in failure, they will be defamed in the history books as traitors. On the other hand, if they succeed and the government is overthrown, their names will be remembered in history as heroes who took a stand against tyranny.

YOUTH: Because history is always written by the victor?

PHILOSOPHER: It is the same with us as individuals. Every person is a compiler of a story of "me," who rewrites his or her own past as desired to prove the legitimacy of "me now."

YOUTH: No! It's different with the individual. The individual's past, and memory, is the domain of neuroscience. Stay out of it! An outdated philosopher like you has no business there.

PHILOSOPHER: With regard to memory, think of it like this: From the innumerable events that have happened in a person's past, that person chooses only those events that are compatible with their present goals, gives meaning to them, and turns them into memories. And conversely, events that run counter to the present goals are erased.

YOUTH: Huh?

PHILOSOPHER: Okay, I'll give you an example from my counseling. Once, a man I was counseling recalled an incident from his childhood in which a dog attacked him and bit his leg. Apparently, his mother had often told him, "If you see a stray dog, stay completely still. Because if you run, it will chase you." There used to be a lot of stray dogs roaming the streets, you see. So one day he came across a stray dog on the side of the road. A friend who had been walking with him ran away, but he obeyed his mother's instructions and stayed rooted to the spot. And the dog attacked him and bit his leg.

YOUTH: Are you saying that memory was a lie that he fabricated?

PHILOSOPHER: It was not a lie. It is probably true that he was bitten. However, there must have been more to the story. After several sessions of counseling, the continuation came back to him. While he was crouching down in pain after getting bitten by the dog, a man who happened to be riding by on a bicycle stopped, helped him get up, and took him straight to the hospital.

In the early stages of counseling, his lifestyle (worldview) had been that "the world is a perilous place, and people are my enemies." To this man, the memory of having been bitten by a dog was an event signifying that this world is a place full of danger. However, once he had begun, little by little, to be able to think, "The world is a safe place, and people are my comrades," episodes that supported that way of thinking started coming back to him.

YOUTH: Hmm.

PHILOSOPHER: Was he bitten by a dog? Or was he helped by another person? The reason Adlerian psychology is considered a "psychology of use" is this aspect of "being able to choose one's own life." The past does not decide now. It is your now that decides the past.

That Bad Person and Poor Me

YOUTH: So, we choose our own lives, and our own pasts?

PHILOSOPHER: Yes. There probably isn't anyone who leads a problem-free life. Every person has sad experiences and setbacks and suffers unbearable treatment and great disappointment. Then why do some people refer to tragedies as "lessons" or "memories," while others remain shackled to such events and regard them as inviolable traumas?

This is not being shackled to the past. That past colored by unhappiness is something one needs. Though it may be putting it harshly, it could be said that one is getting drunk on the cheap wine of tragedy and trying to forget the bitterness of an unfortunate "now."

YOUTH: Enough! You've got some nerve. "Cheap wine of tragedy"? What you're saying is nothing but the logic of the strong, of the victor. You don't know the pain of the downtrodden. You are insulting them.

PHILOSOPHER: No, you are wrong. It is precisely because I believe in human potential that I am opposed to getting drunk on tragedy.

YOUTH: Look, it hasn't been my intention to find out what kind of life you have led, but I think I've started to understand. Basically, without ever having had a major setback or encountering overwhelming irrationality, you have crossed the threshold into a world of nebulous philosophy. That's why you can just brush aside people's emotional scars as if they're nothing. How exceptionally blessed you've been!

PHILOSOPHER: It seems you are having difficulty accepting this. Well, let's give something else a try. This is a triangular column that we use occasionally in counseling.

YOUTH: Sounds interesting. Please explain.

PHILOSOPHER: This triangular column represents our psyche. From where you are sitting right now, you should be able to see only two of the three sides. What is written on those sides?

YOUTH: One side says, "That bad person." The other says, "Poor me."

PHILOSOPHER: Right. Most of the people who come for counseling start off talking about one or the other. They tearfully complain about the unhappiness that has befallen them. Or they speak of their hatred for the people who torment them and the society that surrounds them.

It is not only in counseling that I have encountered this behavior. When speaking with family and friends, or when offering consultation, it is not an easy thing to be conscious of what one is talking about at that moment. However, by visualizing it in this way, one can see clearly that what one is talking about is actually just these two things. It sounds familiar, doesn't it?

YOUTH: To blame "that bad person" or to plead "poor me." Well, I guess you could put it that way. . . .

PHILOSOPHER: But this is not the point we should be talking to each other about. No matter how much you seek agreement regarding "that bad person" or complain about "poor me," regardless of whether there is someone who listens and understands, even if you derive some temporary comfort from it, this will not lead to a true solution.

YOUTH: Then what can one do?

PHILOSOPHER: The triangular column has another side that is hidden from you now. What do you think is written on it?

YOUTH: Hey, stop messing around and just show it to me!

PHILOSOPHER: All right. Please read out loud what it says there.

The philosopher had brought out a piece of paper folded into a triangular column. From where the youth sat, only two of its three faces could be seen. On one face were the words "That bad person," and on the other, "Poor me." According to the philosopher, the complaints of anxious people always ended up being one or the other. And then the philosopher slowly rotated the triangular column with his thin fingers, and revealed the words written on the remaining face—words that shook the youth's heart.

There's No Magic in Adlerian Psychology

YOUTH: ... !!

PHILOSOPHER: Well, say it out loud.

YOUTH: "What should I do from now on?"

PHILOSOPHER: Yes, this is precisely the point we should be talking to each other about: "What should I do from now on?" We do not need "that bad person." Neither is "poor me" necessary. No matter how loudly you complain about them, I will just ignore it.

YOUTH: You, you're inhuman!

PHILOSOPHER: I will not ignore it out of indifference. I will ignore it because there is nothing there that we should talk to each other about. If I were to listen to stories about "that bad person" or "poor me," and sympathize with your plight by saying things like, "That must have been tough," or "It's not your fault at all," it is true that you might get some temporary solace. And you might even have a sense of satisfaction that it was good to get counseling, or good to consult this person.

But how would that change things the next day, and every day after that? Wouldn't you just want to seek more solace the next time you are hurt? Isn't that dependence? That is why, in Adlerian psychology, we talk to each other about "What should one do from now on?"

YOUTH: But if you're saying I should think seriously about my own "from now on," then first I would need to know about "until now," as its precondition.

PHILOSOPHER: No. Right now, you are in front of me. It is enough to know "you who are in front of me," and in principle there is no way for me to know "the past you." I repeat, the past does not exist. The past you speak of is nothing more than a story skillfully compiled by "you now." Please understand this point.

YOUTH: No way! You are just sticking random pieces of theory together and reproaching me to "stop whining." You're just pushing the logic of the arrogant and strong, without any regard for human weakness, without even trying to become familiar with that weakness.

PHILOSOPHER: That is not so. For example, it is not uncommon for us counselors to simply pass this triangular column to the client. And we make the following request: "It does not matter what the subject is, so please turn it to show me the content of what you are going to talk about." At that, many people choose "What should I do from now on?" of their own accord, and then begin thinking about the substance of that.

YOUTH: Of their own accord?

PHILOSOPHER: In other schools of counseling, there are shock therapy–style approaches that attempt to provoke explosions of emotion by tracing deep into the past. But there is absolutely no need to engage in such practices.

We are not prestidigitators or magicians. I repeat, there is no magic in Adlerian psychology. A constructive and scientific psychology of human knowledge that is based not on mysterious magic but on respect for people—that is Adlerian psychology.

YOUTH: . . . Wow, you're going out on a limb again, and using the word "scientific"?

PHILOSOPHER: I am.

YOUTH: All right. I'll swallow that. For the time being, I will allow that. Now, let's get down to talking together about what is really the biggest issue for me: my "from now on." My future as an educator.

PART II
Why Negate Reward and Punishment?

This dialogue with the philosopher wasn't going to be wrapped up so easily, the youth realized. He had to admit it—this old Socrates was a formidable opponent, especially with all the abstract theories he kept bringing up. But the youth still felt sure he would win in the end. *Take the discussion out of this little study as soon as possible and bring it to the classroom. Put it to the test in the real world. I don't want to just criticize it haphazardly. But it's just a bunch of pie-in-the-sky theories that are totally divorced from reality, and I want to bring it all down to earth, into people's actual lives.* The youth pulled up a chair and took a deep breath.

The Classroom Is a
Democratic Nation

YOUTH: In this world, the past does not exist. One must not get drunk on the cheap wine of tragedy. The only thing we should be talking to each other about is "What should be done from now on?" Okay, I'll go along with this premise. The issue I'll be facing from now on, I suppose, is the kind of teaching I put into practice in my school. So I'm going to get into this area of discussion right away. You're okay with that, right?

PHILOSOPHER: Of course.

YOUTH: All right. Earlier you said that the concrete first step is to "start from respect," right? This is what I want to ask you. Do you think that just by bringing respect into the classroom, that will solve everything? In other words, that the students will stop making any trouble?

PHILOSOPHER: That won't solve things on its own. There will still be trouble.

YOUTH: Then I'll have to yell at them after all, won't I? Because they're still engaging in bad conduct and being a nuisance to other students.

PHILOSOPHER: No, you must not rebuke them.

YOUTH: So you're saying I should just let them do bad things right under my nose, and not do anything about it? But that's no different from saying that a thief shouldn't be caught and punished, now is it? Would Adler accept such lawlessness?

PHILOSOPHER: Adler's view is not one that ignores laws or rules. That is, as long as they are rules that have been created through a democratic process. This is an extremely important point, both for society as a whole, and for running a classroom.

YOUTH: A democratic process?

PHILOSOPHER: Yes. Think of your classroom as a democratic nation.

YOUTH: Huh, what do you mean?

PHILOSOPHER: The principle of "national sovereignty" is that "sovereign power rests with the people." The people then establish all manner of rules on the basis of mutual consent, and those rules are applied equally to all citizens. And so, rather than simply obeying the rules, they can observe them more actively as "our rules."

On the other hand, what happens when rules are established according to someone's solitary judgment, rather than on the basis of citizen consensus, and when, furthermore, those rules are enforced very unequally?

YOUTH: Well, you can bet the people won't be quiet about it.

PHILOSOPHER: Then to suppress a rebellion, the ruler would have no choice but to exercise tangible and intangible "powers." This is something that concerns not only the nation, but the corporation and the family too. An organization in which someone is using their power to suppress has irrationality at its foundation.

YOUTH: Hmm. I see.

PHILOSOPHER: The same goes for the classroom. The sovereign of the classroom-nation is not the teacher, it's the students. And the rules of the classroom must be established on the basis of consensus from the students, who are sovereign. Let us start with this principle in mind.

YOUTH: As usual, you're making things very complicated. So, what you're saying is that the students should be allowed to govern themselves? Our school already has a regular system of self-government in place, with a student council and such.

PHILOSOPHER: No, I am talking about something more fundamental. If, for example, we think of the classroom as a nation, then the students are the "citizens." What would be the position of the teacher, then?

YOUTH: Well, if you're saying the students are the citizens, I suppose the teacher would be the prime minister or president who acts as their leader.

PHILOSOPHER: But that doesn't seem right, does it? Were you chosen by the students in an election? And if you were to call yourself a president without having gone through an election, it wouldn't be a democratic nation. It would just be a dictatorship.

YOUTH: I guess so. Logically speaking, anyway.

PHILOSOPHER: I am not talking about logic, but about reality. The classroom is not a dictatorship that is ruled over by the teacher. It is a democratic nation in which each and every student is sovereign. Teachers who forget this principle set up a dictatorship without even realizing it.

YOUTH: Ha-ha! So you're saying I've got fascistic leanings?

PHILOSOPHER: If you put it in extreme terms, yes. The fact that your classroom has gotten out of control is not the problem of your students individually. And you are not insufficiently qualified as a teacher. It is only that the situation there is akin to a corrupted dictatorship—that is why it is out of control. An organization that is under the command of a dictator cannot escape corruption.

YOUTH: Stop making accusations! On what grounds can you make such criticisms?

PHILOSOPHER: The grounds are quite clear. It is that "reward and punishment," which you insist is necessary.

YOUTH: What are you talking about!?

PHILOSOPHER: This is what you came to talk to me about, yes? The subject of praising and rebuking.

YOUTH: . . . It's funny that you're the one who's throwing down the gauntlet! I've gained a fair amount of teaching experience, especially in real classrooms. I'm going to make you take back those extremely rude accusations, you can count on it!

PHILOSOPHER: All right, let's talk it over to our hearts' content.

Do Not Rebuke and Do Not Praise

YOUTH: Adler forbids reward and punishment. He advises not to rebuke, and not to praise. Why did Adler espouse such nonsense? And did he realize how much of a gap there is between the ideal and the reality? That is what I want to know.

PHILOSOPHER: I see. Just to make sure, you think of rebuking and praising as both being necessary?

YOUTH: Yes, of course I do. Even if my students might not like me because of it, I still have to rebuke them. They have to correct their mistakes. Yes, let's start with whether rebuking is right or wrong.

PHILOSOPHER: All right. Why must one not rebuke a person? It is probably best to look at this according to the situation. First, consider a boy who has done something bad. It could be something dangerous or that might harm another person, or something approaching a criminal act. Why on earth did the boy do such a thing? One thing that may be considered, then, is the possibility that he did not know it was a bad thing.

YOUTH: He didn't know?

PHILOSOPHER: Right. I'll use my own story as an example. When I was a child, I had a magnifying glass with me wherever I went. I'd find insects and plants and look at them through it. I passed the time gazing to my heart's content at worlds that were invisible to the naked eye. I'd spend all day absorbed in observing them, like a little entomologist.

YOUTH: Yes, I had such a phase too.

PHILOSOPHER: A little while later, though, I learned of a completely different use for the magnifying glass. I'd focus the sunlight through it onto a piece of black paper, and lo and behold, smoke would rise from the paper, until at last it would begin to burn. Witnessing this miracle of science that seemed like a magic trick, I felt the excitement course through me, and I couldn't think of it as a magnifying glass anymore.

YOUTH: It's really something, isn't it? I too found that more to my liking, more so than crawling around on the ground staring at bugs. A small magnifying glass may inspire one to contemplate the power of the sun, and even contemplate the universe. It's a boy's first step into science.

PHILOSOPHER: So, I was playing in this way one hot summer day, by burning paper. I'd placed a sheet of black paper on the ground, and I was focusing the light with my magnifying glass as I always did, when out of the corner of my eye I caught sight of a solitary ant. It was a large and sturdy ant with a deep black exoskeleton. I was getting bored already with the black paper, so what did I do to the black ant with my magnifying glass? . . . I don't think I need to explain any further.

YOUTH: . . . I get it. Well, children can be cruel.

PHILOSOPHER: Yes. Children often do exhibit this sort of brutality, of killing insects for fun. But are children really cruel? Do they walk around with some latent "aggressive behavior," as Freud calls it? I don't think so. Children are not cruel—it's just that they don't know. They do not know what life is worth, or about other people's pain.

So, there is one thing that adults should do. If children do not know, teach them. And when teaching them, there is no need for words of reprimand. Please do not forget this principle. Because it is not that they were engaging in bad behavior, but simply that they did not know.

YOUTH: You're saying that it's not aggression or brutality, but a crime arising from ignorance?

PHILOSOPHER: A child playing on railroad tracks might not realize that it is a dangerous thing to do. A child shouting loudly in a public place might not know he is causing a disturbance. Whatever it may be, we all start from a point of "not knowing." Wouldn't you say that it is unreasonable to sternly reproach someone, if they do not know that what they are doing is wrong?

YOUTH: Sure, if they really do not know.

PHILOSOPHER: What is needed of us adults is not to reprimand, but to teach. With words of reason, and without getting emotional or raising our voices. You are not someone who cannot do this.

YOUTH: If that were the only example, then it'd be just as you say. Because there's no way you're going to accept your own ant-killing brutality, right!? But this isn't a line of reasoning that I'll ever swallow. It just feels like it'll get stuck in the back of my throat, like thick maple syrup or something. Your understanding of people is too naive.

PHILOSOPHER: What is naive about it?

YOUTH: Kindergartners are one thing. But when it comes to grammar-school children, and even more so with middle schoolers, they're all fully aware of what they're doing. They've known for a long time what's prohibited and what's considered immoral. You might say that these kids engage in problem behavior as prisoners of conscience. They've got to be severely punished for their offenses. So I wish you would just dispense with this old-man act of making them out to be a bunch of pure-hearted angels!

PHILOSOPHER: To be sure, there are many children who engage in problem behavior knowing full well that it is wrong. And that may even be the case for the majority of them. But haven't you ever found it odd? They're engaging in problem behavior not only with the knowledge that it is "wrong," but with the understanding that they will be rebuked by their parents and teachers for acting out. It's quite irrational.

YOUTH: It's simplistic, that's what it is. They would understand if they'd only calm down and think it over, but they're incapable of that.

PHILOSOPHER: But is that really the case? Can't you see that there is another mentality operating deep inside them?

YOUTH: So they do it knowing that they're going to be rebuked? Even the kids who cry when they're rebuked?

PHILOSOPHER: It would not be a waste of effort to consider that possibility, certainly. In contemporary Adlerian psychology, we think of human problem behavior as having five stages, each of which has its own mental state operating in the background.

YOUTH: Oh, you're finally getting to the psychology!

PHILOSOPHER: Once you comprehend the five stages of problem behavior, you should be able to see for yourself whether rebuking is right or wrong.

YOUTH: Let's hear it, then. And I'm going to see how much you really comprehend children, and the actual educational setting!

This philosopher's reasoning makes no sense at all! The youth had become incensed. *The classroom is a small democratic nation. And the sovereigns of the classroom are the students. Fine up to that point. But why are reward and punishment unnecessary? If the classroom is a nation, aren't laws needed there? And if there are people who break laws and commit crimes, aren't punishments needed?* The youth wrote the words "The five stages of problem behavior" in his notebook and smiled to himself. *I am going to ascertain if Adlerian psychology is an area of study that actually holds water in the real world, or if it's just a bunch of empty theories.*

What Is the Goal of
Problem Behavior?

PHILOSOPHER: Why do children get involved in problem behavior? Adlerian psychology focuses on the goals that lie hidden in that behavior. That is to say, we think of the problem behavior that children (and adults) engage in, with all manner of goals, as having five stages.

YOUTH: Does having five stages mean it is something that gradually escalates?

PHILOSOPHER: Yes. And these stages cover all forms of human problem behavior. When possible, steps must be taken at an early stage before the behavior escalates.

YOUTH: All right. So, what is the first stage?

PHILOSOPHER: The first stage of problem behavior is "demand for admiration."

YOUTH: Demand for admiration? In other words, it's as if they're saying, "Praise me"?

PHILOSOPHER: Yes. At this stage, students play the role of the "good child" to their parents and teachers, and to others. A person working in an organization strives to demonstrate their drive and obedience to their boss and senior colleagues. By doing so, they hope to gain their praise. This is where it all starts.

YOUTH: But isn't that desirable behavior? They're being productive and not causing trouble for anyone. They can make themselves useful to other people. I can't find any reason to regard this as problematic.

PHILOSOPHER: Certainly, if each of their actions is treated as separate, they may appear to be "good children" or "honor students" who have no problems whatsoever. And with children who make great efforts in their schoolwork and athletics and such, or with company employees who devote themselves to their work, they are applying themselves, so one wants to praise them.

There is a great pitfall here, however. Their goal will always be "to receive praise," and moreover, "to gain a privileged position within the community."

YOUTH: Aha. So, since their motives aren't pure, they're unacceptable? What a simpleminded philosopher you are. Even if their goal is to receive praise, they're still students pursuing their studies, aren't they? I don't see any problem here.

PHILOSOPHER: Then what do you think happens when their efforts garner no praise at all from their parents and teachers, or their bosses and coworkers?

YOUTH: . . . I suppose they become dissatisfied, and maybe even resentful.

PHILOSOPHER: Right. Think of it this way: they are not doing "good things"; they are "seeking praise." And there is no point in making so much effort if they are not going to be praised or treated in a special way. So they lose motivation right away.

They adopt a lifestyle, or worldview, in which they are essentially saying, "I won't engage in proper behavior unless there is someone who will praise me," and "I'll engage in improper behavior unless there is someone who will punish me."

YOUTH: Well, I guess that's true, but—

PHILOSOPHER: Furthermore, another characteristic of this stage is that, on account of trying to be the good child who is full of promise, they begin to engage in cheating, deceptive tactics and other wrongdoing. Educators and leaders must ascertain the children's goals instead of focusing only on their actions.

YOUTH: But if you don't praise them at that point, they'll lose their drive and turn into children who don't do anything at all. And in some cases, they'll start engaging in improper behavior, won't they?

PHILOSOPHER: No. You teach them continually that they have worth, even if they are not "special," by showing them respect.

YOUTH: Concretely speaking, how do you do that?

PHILOSOPHER: Instead of focusing on whenever a child does some "good thing," turn your attention to the smaller everyday details of their words and actions. And then focus on and sympathize with that person's concerns. That's all.

YOUTH: Ah, so we're back to that. Well, I guess I still don't feel comfortable with what qualifies as problem behavior. But let's move on. What about the second stage?

PHILOSOPHER: The second stage of problem behavior is "attention drawing."

YOUTH: Attention drawing?

PHILOSOPHER: The child isn't being praised, even though they have done a good thing. They are unable to gain a privileged position within the classroom. Or they don't have enough courage or tenacity to follow through with "being praised" in the first place. At such times, the person thinks, "It's okay not to be praised, so I'll just make myself stand out."

YOUTH: So, they will do something bad? Something they will get rebuked for?

PHILOSOPHER: That's right. At this stage, they don't even think about being praised anymore. They just want to stand out. One aspect I would like you to bear in mind here is that the principle of the behavior of children at this stage is "standing out," not "being bad."

YOUTH: What will they accomplish by standing out?

PHILOSOPHER: They want to gain a privileged position within the classroom. They want a definite "place to be" within the community to which they belong. That is their true goal.

YOUTH: In other words, since orthodox methods such as doing their schoolwork haven't worked out, the student tries to become a "special me" by other means. Instead of becoming special as a good child, they try to do so as a bad child. In this way, they secure their own place to be.

PHILOSOPHER: That's exactly right.

YOUTH: Well, I'd say that at around that age, if you're a bit of a bad child, you're more likely to be viewed as superior. So, concretely speaking, in what way do they make themselves stand out?

PHILOSOPHER: Assertive children will probably try to get attention by "mischief"; that is to say, by breaking the lesser rules of society and school. Being noisy in class, ridiculing the teacher, inundating the teacher with endless questions—that kind of thing. But they never go so far as to incur the wrath of the adults, and they are often loved by their teachers and friends alike as a kind of popular class clown.

Passive children will probably try to get attention by exhibiting a dramatic drop in scholastic achievement, by repeatedly forgetting things, or by crying. They get attention by acting like an "incompetent child," and try to gain a special position.

YOUTH: But if they do things like disrupting class or repeatedly forgetting things, they'll probably be rebuked quite severely. Are they okay with being rebuked?

PHILOSOPHER: If their presence is likely to be otherwise ignored, they would much rather be rebuked. They want their presence recognized, and they want to be put in a special position, even if it takes the form of rebuke. That is their wish.

YOUTH: Oh my, that's harsh! What a complicated frame of mind.

PHILOSOPHER: No, actually, children up to this second stage are living according to a simple principle, and dealing with them is not so difficult. Through respect we can convey that there is no need to be special, and that they have sufficient worth just as they are. It is from the third stage onward that things get difficult.

YOUTH: Hmm. Why is that, I wonder?

Hate Me! Abandon Me!

PHILOSOPHER: In the third stage of problem behavior, their goals plunge into "power struggles."

YOUTH: Power struggles?

PHILOSOPHER: Yielding to no one, repeated provocation, and challenging others to battle. By winning that battle, each one tries to make a show of his own "might." Each one tries to gain a privileged position. This is a quite tough stage.

YOUTH: What do you mean by challenging others to battle? They don't actually start hitting each other, do they?

PHILOSOPHER: In a word, it is "resistance." They provoke their parents and teachers and swear at them. Sometimes they become enraged and violent, or run around engaging in shoplifting and smoking cigarettes and the like, and they will break rules without a second thought.

YOUTH: Well, they're the real problem children. Yes, these are exactly the sort of kids I feel helpless dealing with.

PHILOSOPHER: Passive children, on the other hand, will challenge one to a power struggle through "disobedience." No matter how much they are rebuked with stern words, they will refuse to engage in their studies or lessons. They will pretend to ignore the words of the adults. They don't particularly want to study, but they don't feel that study is unnecessary, either. It is simply that they want to prove their own might by being resolutely disobedient.

YOUTH: Ah, it's infuriating just imagining it! There's no way to handle such problem children other than by yelling at them! They really are breaking the rules, and it makes me want to just give them a good smack. Because if I don't, I'm essentially condoning their misdeeds.

PHILOSOPHER: Right. Many parents and teachers choose to reprimand their children and students in anger. But this is nothing more than giving in to the provocation of the other, and standing on the same court with them. They will be only too glad to respond with resistance. Because their battle has just begun.

YOUTH: So, what can be done about it?

PHILOSOPHER: If there is a legal issue, then it must be dealt with in a legal manner. With any other power struggle, however, get off the battlefield as soon as you detect it.

That's the only thing you should do right away. Consider that even without making reprimands, just by looking like you're about to get angry, you will end up standing on the battlefield of the power struggle.

YOUTH: But what if there's a student doing something bad right in front of me!? What do I do about this in real life? Is an educator someone who just leaves the student alone and doesn't do anything?

PHILOSOPHER: I am sure there is a single logical conclusion, but it would be better to wait until I have explained all five stages before we think it over together.

YOUTH: Ugh, how annoying. Next!

PHILOSOPHER: The fourth stage of problem behavior is the one where the person plunges into the stage of "revenge."

YOUTH: Revenge?

PHILOSOPHER: They have made up their mind to enter a power struggle, but it was beyond their ability. They are unable to win a victory or gain a privileged position. They are snubbed by others and suffer a defeat. Having lost the battle in this way, the person withdraws temporarily, and then plots revenge.

YOUTH: Who do they take revenge on, and for what purpose?

PHILOSOPHER: They take love's revenge on those who would not recognize the irreplaceable "me," on those who would not love them.

YOUTH: Love's revenge?

PHILOSOPHER: Please remember—demand for admiration, attention drawing, and power struggles are all expressions of the love-starved feeling that says, "I want you to have greater regard for me." The thing is, the moment that a person realizes that their longing for love will not be fulfilled, they do an about-face and begin to look for "hate."

YOUTH: Why? What is the point of looking for hate?

PHILOSOPHER: "I realize now that they aren't going to love me. If that's how it's going to be, then hate me. Pay attention to me, within that emotion of hatred." This is the kind of thing they think.

YOUTH: . . . They wish to be hated?

PHILOSOPHER: That is what happens. Take, for example, the children of the third stage who oppose their parents and teachers and challenge them to power struggles. In the classroom, they have a chance of becoming minor heroes—of being celebrated for their courage to stand up to authority, and to adults.

But children who plunge into the stage of revenge are not celebrated by anyone. Hated and feared by their parents and teachers, and even their classmates, little by little they become isolated. Even so, they try to connect with others through that one point of "being hated."

YOUTH: If that's how it is, we should just pretend to ignore them! Just break that point of contact, which has become hateful! Because there won't be any need for revenge that way. We can figure out some other, more sensible approach, can't we?

PHILOSOPHER: That might work in theory. But in reality, it is quite difficult to tolerate their conduct.

YOUTH: Why is that? Are you saying that I don't have the patience for it?

PHILOSOPHER: With children in the power struggles stage, for example, they will challenge one to battle head-on, fair and square. Their provocations, which bristle with abusive language, are directly related to their sense of justice. That is why they may be seen as heroes by their classmates. It is possible to deal with this kind of provocation in a calm way.

With children in the stage of revenge, on the other hand, one does not choose to fight them directly. They are not planning to do "bad things." They are just repeating "things that other people don't like."

YOUTH: . . . Could you give me a concrete example?

PHILOSOPHER: An obvious one would be what is known as stalking behavior, which is a typical form of revenge. It is love's revenge, aimed at the person who would not love you. People who become stalkers are well aware that their target will not like their behavior. And they are aware that good relations cannot come out of it. But they will still plot to connect in some way through "hatred" or "dislike."

YOUTH: What kind of unpleasant logic is that!?

PHILOSOPHER: Self-harm and social withdrawal are also considered to be within the realm of revenge in Adlerian psychology. By engaging in harm to oneself and injury to one's worth, one accuses the other, saying, "It's your fault I've ended up this way." Naturally, the child's parents will worry, and it will be a heart-wrenching experience for them. From the child's point of view, the revenge is succeeding.

YOUTH: . . . Well, we're venturing into the domain of the psychiatrist now, aren't we? Any other examples?

PHILOSOPHER: While we often hear about cases that escalate to violence or abusive language, there are also many problem children who get involved with groups of delinquents or with organized crime. And with passive children, there are all kinds of methods of revenge, such as letting themselves get abnormally dirty, or indulging in grotesque habits that are sure to arouse feelings of dislike in those around them.

YOUTH: What should we do when confronted with such children?

PHILOSOPHER: If there are students like this in your classroom, there is nothing you can do about it. Their goal is "revenge on you." The more you try to give them a helping hand, the more their words and actions will escalate, as they will only see it as an opportunity for revenge. At this point, the only thing to do is request assistance from a completely outside party who has no interest in the situation whatsoever. In other words, you would have no choice but to turn to another teacher, or to people outside the school—including specialists like me, for example.

YOUTH: . . . But, if this is the fourth stage, there's something beyond it, right?

PHILOSOPHER: Yes. There is the final stage, which is even more trouble-some than revenge.

YOUTH: Please tell me.

PHILOSOPHER: The fifth stage of problem behavior is "proof of incompetence."

YOUTH: Proof of incompetence?

PHILOSOPHER: That's right. Here, please try to think about it as if it were you yourself. Though you have taken all sorts of steps to ensure that you will be treated as a "special being," none of them is going as planned. Your parents and teachers, and even your classmates, are not hating you as you wish them to. You cannot find a "place to be" in either the classroom or at home. . . . What would you do, if this were you?

YOUTH: I'd probably give up right away. Because no matter what I do, I can't get anyone to acknowledge me. I guess I'd just stop making any effort at all.

PHILOSOPHER: Still, your parents and teachers would lecture you that you need to study more, and they would start intervening in various things, such as your attitude in school and your relationships with friends. Because they want to help you, of course.

YOUTH: It's none of their business! If they could do it right, they could've done it a long time ago. I'd wish they wouldn't care at all.

PHILOSOPHER: You won't be able to get them to understand that. The people around you want you to try harder. They know you can do things, and they are expecting you to change through your own work on yourself.

YOUTH: What I'm saying is that sort of expectation is a big nuisance! I'd want them to leave me alone.

PHILOSOPHER: . . . That's right. It's that feeling of "don't expect anything more of me" that connects to "proof of incompetence."

YOUTH: So, what they're saying is, "Don't expect anything of me, because I'm incompetent"?

PHILOSOPHER: Yes. They start to despair of life, they despise themselves from the bottom of their heart, and they firmly believe that they can't solve anything. So, in order to avoid experiencing any more despair, they try to run away from all their schoolwork. They are announcing to those around them: "This is how incompetent I am, so don't give me any assignments. I don't have the ability to complete them."

YOUTH: They do this in order to not get hurt anymore?

PHILOSOPHER: That's right. If they think, "Maybe I can do it" when they undertake an assignment, and then end up failing to complete it, they will wish they had decided, "There's no way I can do it" at the outset, and just given up. Because it would be easier that way, and there would be no worry of being further overcome with disappointment.

YOUTH: . . . Well, I can understand the feeling.

PHILOSOPHER: Then by various means they try to prove how incompetent they are. They act as if they are utter fools, become lethargic about everything, and stop trying to undertake even the easiest assignments. Eventually, they convince even themselves of being "me the fool."

YOUTH: It's true that there are students who say they're stupid.

PHILOSOPHER: If they can put it into words, they are probably just making fun of themselves. With children who are really in the fifth stage, while they are acting like utter fools, they may appear to actually be suffering some mental illness. Whenever they find themselves trying to do their work or trying to think about things, they immediately stop themselves. And then they pessimistically reject their assignments and the expectations of those around them.

YOUTH: How should we interact with such children?

PHILOSOPHER: What they are wishing is "Don't expect anything of me," "Don't care about me," and even "Abandon me." The more their parents and teachers try to help them, the more they will demonstrate proof of incompetence in extreme ways. Unfortunately, there is nothing you can do. You will just have to turn to a specialist. Because even for a specialist, the path of providing assistance to children who have entered the proof of incompetence stage is a very difficult one.

YOUTH: . . . There's not much we educators can do for them.

PHILOSOPHER: Actually, the majority of problem behaviors can be stopped during the power struggles of the third stage. So, the role given to educators is a major one in preventing those behaviors from progressing further.

If There Is Punishment, Does the Crime Go Away?

YOUTH: The five stages of problem behavior . . . It certainly is an interesting analysis. First, you look for admiration. Then you go all-out to get people's attention. When that doesn't work, you start power struggles, which then turn into heinous revenge. And lastly, you make a show of your own incompetence.

PHILOSOPHER: And all of these are rooted in a "sense of belonging"; that is to say, the goal of "securing a special position within the community."

YOUTH: Right. That is a very Adlerian psychology–style, interpersonal relationship–focused line of reasoning. Let's acknowledge this classification.

But have you forgotten? Shouldn't we be discussing whether rebuking is right or wrong? Look, I have put this Adlerian "no-rebuking education" into practice. I have waited, without rebuking no matter what, for them to notice things on their own. And what do you think has happened to my class as a result? It's turned into a complete zoo, without any rules whatsoever!

PHILOSOPHER: So, you chose rebuking. Did anything change by rebuking?

YOUTH: If I yell at the students in a loud voice when they're being noisy, things quiet down right away. And if I rebuke them when they forget to do their homework, they get looks of self-reflection on their faces. It doesn't last, though. They start making noise again in short order, and they stop doing their homework too.

PHILOSOPHER: Why do you think it happens this way?

YOUTH: I'm telling you, it's because of Adler! It was a mistake to decide to start with no rebuking. Since I started off by being easygoing and allowing everything, they look down on me now and think, "This guy's nothing to be afraid of" and "He'll let us get away with anything"!

PHILOSOPHER: Would it have been different if you'd been rebuking from the start?

YOUTH: Of course it would have. This is my greatest regret. In everything, the way you start is crucial. Next year, if I get assigned to a different classroom, I'm going to start yelling at them strictly from the very first day.

PHILOSOPHER: So, there are some very strict people among your coworkers and senior colleagues, aren't there?

YOUTH: Yes. Well, no one goes as far as corporal punishment, of course. But there are several teachers who always yell at their students and instruct them using strict language. They put everything they have into playing the bad guy, into the role of the teacher. I guess you could say they are paragons of the professional educator.

PHILOSOPHER: Well, that's strange. Why are these teachers "always" yelling?

YOUTH: Why? Because the students do bad things.

PHILOSOPHER: No, because if rebuking were effective as an educational approach, just doing it a few times at the outset should be enough to put a stop to the problem behavior. Why do they end up "always" rebuking?

Why do they "always" put on a scary face, and "always" use a loud voice? Hasn't it ever seemed odd to you?

YOUTH: But it's because those kids are so impossible!

PHILOSOPHER: No, you are wrong. This is undeniable proof that rebuking is not effective in any way as an educational approach. Even if you were to engage in strict rebuking from the start next year, the situation would not be any different from now. It might actually be worse.

YOUTH: It'd be worse!?

PHILOSOPHER: You should understand by now that their problem behavior is such in which "being rebuked by you" is implied. It is their wish to be reprimanded.

YOUTH: They wish to be rebuked by their teacher? They enjoy it? Ha-ha, now they're masochists. Stop joking around!

PHILOSOPHER: I wouldn't say that anyone enjoys being rebuked. But there is a sense of heroic fulfillment in being able to say to oneself, "I did something that was *special enough to get rebuked*." They can prove to themselves that they are special beings by getting rebuked.

YOUTH: No, before being a question of human psychology, this is a question of law and order. There's someone doing something bad right in front of you. Regardless of what goal might be involved, that person is breaking a rule. It is only natural to punish them for that. If that is not done, the public order cannot be maintained.

PHILOSOPHER: You are rebuking in order to maintain law and order?

YOUTH: That's right. It's not that I want to rebuke my students. And I don't want to punish them either. It's obvious—who would want to do that kind of thing! . . . But punishment is necessary. One reason is to maintain law and order. And another is as a deterrence against crime.

PHILOSOPHER: What do you mean by "deterrence"?

YOUTH: A boxer in the ring, for example, even if he finds himself in a tight spot with no way out, will never kick at or try to throw his opponent, no matter what. Because he knows full well that he'll be disqualified if he does anything like that. So, the grave punishment—disqualification—functions as a deterrence against rule violation. If the administering of that punishment is inconsistent, it will no longer act as a deterrence, and the boxing match will no longer exist as such. Punishment is the only deterrence against crime.

PHILOSOPHER: It is an interesting example. Then why don't such serious punishments—in other words, the reprimands all of you are giving—function as a deterrence in an actual education setting?

YOUTH: There are all kinds of opinions about that. The senior teachers all reminisce about the old days when corporal punishment was allowed. Basically, they say that times have changed, and because punishment has gotten lighter it has lost its function as a deterrence.

PHILOSOPHER: I see. Now, let's probe a little deeper into why rebuking cannot have any effectiveness as an educational approach.

The five stages of problem behavior conveyed by the philosopher—to be sure, the truths they contained were accurate assessments of human psychology and offered glimpses of the greatness of Adler. *Still*, the youth thought, *I am the only adult in charge of my classroom, and it is up to me to set an example as a person living in society. In other words, if punishment is not meted out to those who engage in wrongdoing, the order of this "society" will fall apart. I am not a philosopher who uses theories to treat people like playthings—I am an educator who bears responsibility for our children's future. This weight, this responsibility for people living in the real world, is not something this man is capable of understanding!*

Violence in the Name of Communication

YOUTH: So, where do we begin?

PHILOSOPHER: All right. Let's suppose that a violent fight breaks out between two students in your classroom. A quarrel over something trivial has developed into a full-scale fistfight. What would you do with them?

YOUTH: In that sort of situation, I would not rebuke them loudly, or anything like that. Rather, I'd calmly listen to what both sides had to say. I'd get them to cool down first, and then ask them things like, "Why did you start fighting?" and "Why were you hitting each other?"

PHILOSOPHER: How do you think they would answer?

YOUTH: Well, I guess it'd be something like, "He said such-and-such, and I just blew up," or "He did this horrible thing to me."

PHILOSOPHER: Then what would you do?

YOUTH: I'd let them both have their say, ascertain which student was in the wrong, and then get that one to apologize. However, since in all disputes it's really both sides that are in the wrong, I'd actually be getting them to apologize to each other.

PHILOSOPHER: Would they be satisfied with that?

YOUTH: Naturally, they'd both prefer to stick to their versions of what happened. But if both of them are able to think, *Maybe it's partly my fault*, I would let it go at that. There's that saying, "In a quarrel both parties are to blame."

PHILOSOPHER: I see. Now, suppose you had that triangular column with you.

YOUTH: The triangular column?

PHILOSOPHER: Yes. On one face are written the words "That bad person," on another "Poor me," and on the last one "What should I do from now on?" Listen to your students while visualizing the triangular column, in much the same way that we counselors do.

YOUTH: How do you mean?

PHILOSOPHER: The students' reasons for fighting: "He said such-and-such" and "He did this horrible thing to me." When you think about them with the triangular column, isn't it just the same as "That bad person" and "Poor me"?

YOUTH: ... Yes, I guess so.

PHILOSOPHER: You're asking the students only about the cause. No matter how much you might delve into that, all you're going to get is excuses and abdications of responsibility. What you should be doing is focusing on their goals, and thinking with them, "What should I do from now on?"

YOUTH: The goal of the fight? Not the cause?

PHILOSOPHER: Let's figure this out step by step. First of all, we humans usually communicate through language, right?

YOUTH: Yes. Like we are talking to each other right now.

PHILOSOPHER: Then what would you say is the goal, or objective, of communication?

YOUTH: I'd say it's transmission of intention—the conveying of what is on one's mind.

PHILOSOPHER: No. "Conveying" is nothing more than the gateway of communication. The final objective is the establishment of consensus. Conveying does not have meaning on its own. It is only when the content of what is conveyed has been understood and a certain consensus has been reached that communication has meaning. So, we are talking together in this way with the aim of getting to some point of consensus.

YOUTH: Okay, but it's sure taking a long time!

PHILOSOPHER: Right. Language-based communication necessitates a great deal of time and effort to arrive at consensus. One doesn't just get one's own egotistical demands accepted. Rather, one has to collect persuasive material, such as objective data. Moreover, in terms of certainty and immediate effectiveness, it is rather poor for the costs incurred.

YOUTH: It's exactly as you say. It gets tiresome.

PHILOSOPHER: What does the person who is finding a discussion tiresome, or feeling that they have no chance of winning the discussion, do at that point? Do you know?

YOUTH: Well, I suppose they wouldn't just bow out, would they?

PHILOSOPHER: The means of communication they will choose in the end is violence.

YOUTH: Ha-ha! That's great! That's where you make the connection?

PHILOSOPHER: By resorting to violence, one can push through one's demands without expending time or effort. To put it more directly, one can make the other party submit to one. In every way, violence is a low-cost, easy means of communication. But before deeming it morally unacceptable, we must say that it is a rather immature form of conduct for people to engage in.

YOUTH: You mean that it should not be rejected from a moral viewpoint, but rather because it is immature, foolish conduct?

PHILOSOPHER: Yes. Moral standards change with each time period or situation. Judging others solely on moral guidelines is extremely dangerous. After all, there have been times when violence is promoted. Now, what should one do? We humans have to get back to the basics: we must grow out of our immature condition. We must not rely on violence to communicate; rather, we have to search for other kinds of communication. It does not matter what the cause may be, whether it is the thing the other person said, or their provocative attitude, or what have you. Violence has only one goal. What we should be thinking about is: "What should I do from now on?"

YOUTH: I see. That's an interesting insight with regard to violence.

PHILOSOPHER: Can you really act as if this were just someone else's business? What I am talking about can be applied to you too.

YOUTH: No way, I don't engage in violence. Stop making strange accusations!

Getting Angry and Rebuking Are Synonymous

PHILOSOPHER: You're in a discussion with someone, when things take a bad turn. You're in a disadvantageous position. Or you were aware from the start of the discussion that your arguments lack rationality.

Take, for example, the man who tries to push his arguments at such times, not with actual violence perhaps, but through attempting to coerce the other party, by raising his voice, slapping his hand on the table, or shedding tears. These kinds of conduct too must be regarded as low-cost, "violent" communication. . . . You understand what I am saying, yes?

YOUTH: . . . You, you damn insect! Just because I'm getting excited and raising my voice, you ridicule me by calling me an immature person!?

PHILOSOPHER: No, I really don't mind at all how much you raise your voice here. The issue I am bringing up is the essence of the rebuking conduct that you are choosing.

You feel annoyed by communicating with your students with words, and you are rebuking them to try to force them into quick submission. Using anger as a weapon, wielding guns of reproach, brandishing the sword of authority. This is an immature and foolish attitude for an educator to have.

YOUTH: No! I am not angry at them—I am rebuking them!

PHILOSOPHER: Many adults justify it this way. But it does not change the fact that they are trying to keep another person down by using violent force. Indeed, one might even say it is a vicious excuse, as it contains the awareness of those adults who tell themselves, "I am doing a good thing."

YOUTH: That's not how it is! Look, anger is an explosion of emotion, when one cannot make calm judgments. This is what I mean—when I rebuke them, I don't get emotional at all! Instead of getting bent out of shape, I rebuke them in a calm and calculated manner. Don't group me with people who forget themselves and fly into a rage!

PHILOSOPHER: Or maybe that is how it is. You might compare yourself to a gun loaded with blanks, but there is no difference from the standpoint of the students—they have a gun pointing at them. Whether it is loaded with real bullets or not, you are communicating with a gun in your hand.

YOUTH: Okay, let's try this. Suppose the other person is some kind of brutal criminal who's holed up with a knife. He's committed a crime and is challenging you to battle—one of those battles for drawing attention or struggles for power, or what have you. What's wrong with communicating with a gun in your hand? How else do we maintain law and order?

PHILOSOPHER: What should parents and educators do when confronted with problem behavior in children? Adler advises that we "renounce the standpoint of the judge." You have not been granted the privilege of passing down judgments. Maintaining law and order is not your job.

YOUTH: Then what are you telling me to do instead?

PHILOSOPHER: Rather than being concerned with law and order, what you should be doing is protecting the child right in front of you, the child who has engaged in problem behavior. Educators are counselors, and counseling is reeducation. We spoke about this earlier, didn't we? It would be peculiar for a counselor to take out a gun or anything like that.

YOUTH: But, still—

PHILOSOPHER: Violence, which includes reprimand, is a form of communication that reveals one's immaturity as a human being. This is something that the children know well enough themselves. Whenever they receive reprimands, in addition to their fear of violent conduct, at an unconscious level they have the insight that "this is an immature person."

This is a much bigger problem than adults think. Could you respect an immature human being? And could you have a real feeling of being respected by someone who threatens you in a violent manner? There is no respect in communication with anger and violence. Rather, such communication invites contempt. That reprimand does not lead to substantive improvement is a self-evident truth. On this point, Adler states, "Anger is an emotion that pulls people apart."

YOUTH: I am not respected by my students, and moreover, they feel contempt for me? Because of my rebuking them!?

PHILOSOPHER: Unfortunately, that is probably the case.

YOUTH: . . .What do you know, anyway? You don't understand what it's like in a real setting!

PHILOSOPHER: There are probably many things I do not understand. However, this "real setting" that you keep bringing up is basically another version of "that bad person" and the "poor me" who is at their mercy. I do not imagine there to be any more value in those words beyond what is necessary. It will all just go in one ear and out the other.

YOUTH: Argh!

PHILOSOPHER: If you have gained the courage to face yourself and to consider the true meaning of "What should I do from now on?" you will make progress.

YOUTH: So, you are saying that I'm just making excuses?

PHILOSOPHER: No. "Excuse" is probably not the correct word. You are simply focusing only on "the things one cannot change" and lamenting, "So, it's impossible." Instead of clinging to "the things one cannot change," look at "the things one can change" that are right in front of you. . . . Do you remember the Serenity Prayer that has been passed down orally in Christian societies?

YOUTH: Yes, of course, I do. "God, grant me the serenity to accept the things I cannot change, the courage to change the things I can, and wisdom to know the difference."

PHILOSOPHER: Reflect upon these words, and then think once more about "what should I do from now on?"

One Can Choose One's Own Life

YOUTH: Okay, suppose I were to accept your suggestion: I refrain from rebuking, stop inquiring as to the causes of their behavior, and ask the students, "What should you do from now on?" What would be the result? . . . I don't even have to think about it. All I'd get would be lip-service statements of self-reflection, like "I won't do it again," or "I'll do things correctly from now on."

PHILOSOPHER: Whenever words of self-reflection are forced, nothing will come of it. That is to be expected. People are often made to write essays of apology or self-reflection, but their writings are written only with the goal of "being forgiven" and never lead to true self-reflection. It is unlikely that they become anything more than objects of self-satisfaction for the person who had them written. But be that as it may, what I would question here is that person's way of living.

YOUTH: Way of living?

PHILOSOPHER: To paraphrase Kant, whose discussion of self-reliance is pertinent here, "Man's juvenile condition is not due to lack of reason. It is that he has neither the resolution nor the courage to use his reason without direction from another. That is to say, man is responsible for being stuck in his own juvenile condition."

YOUTH: . . . Juvenile condition?

PHILOSOPHER: Yes, it is the condition of not attaining true self-reliance. One may understand Kant's use of the word "reason" as referring to "ability" in general, and to include everything from intelligence to sensibility.

YOUTH: It is not that we lack ability, but that we don't have enough courage to use our ability. And that's why we can't get past our juvenile condition?

PHILOSOPHER: That's right. And then Kant declares, "Have courage to use your own reason!"

YOUTH: Huh, that's just like Adler, isn't it?

PHILOSOPHER: Now, why do people try to keep themselves in a juvenile condition? Or, to put it more plainly, why do people reject self-reliance? What is your view?

YOUTH: . . . Is it because of cowardice?

PHILOSOPHER: It may be, in some cases. But consider Kant's words once more. It is easier to live according to the "direction from another." One does not have to think about difficult things, and one does not have to take responsibility for failure. All one has to do is swear a certain allegiance, and someone will take care of all of one's troublesome tasks—from children in families and schools, to members of society working at companies and government offices, to clients who come for counseling. Isn't it so?

YOUTH: Well, I guess so . . .

PHILOSOPHER: Moreover, in order to keep children in a juvenile condition, the adults around them use every conceivable means to indoctrinate children regarding the dangers, risks, and scariness of self-reliance.

YOUTH: What for?

PHILOSOPHER: To keep them under their control.

YOUTH: Why would they do such a thing?

PHILOSOPHER: This is probably something you should think over carefully and ask yourself. Because without noticing it, you too are getting in the way of your students' self-reliance.

YOUTH: I am!

PHILOSOPHER: Yes, make no mistake about this. No matter what they do, parents, and then educators, engage in excessive meddling with and nurturing of their children. As a result, they end up raising children who cannot decide anything on their own, and who need constant direction from others. They raise people who will always have children's minds, and who will be incapable of doing things without direction from others, even if they are adults in terms of age. This is not self-reliance in any shape or form.

YOUTH: No way. At the very least, I am hoping that my students will become self-reliant! Why would I be actually hindering them?

PHILOSOPHER: Don't you see? You are afraid of letting them become self-reliant.

YOUTH: What! How's that?

PHILOSOPHER: If your students become self-reliant, and they assume a standpoint on equal footing with you, your authority will collapse. Right now, you are erecting a "vertical relationship" with your students, and you are afraid of that relationship collapsing. This is a fear held subconsciously not only by educators, but by many parents as well.

YOUTH: No, I don't . . .

PHILOSOPHER: One other thing. When children fail, and especially when they disturb others, it is only natural that you too are held responsible. It is your responsibility as an educator and as a supervisor, and if you are a parent, it is your responsibility as a parent. Do you see?

YOUTH: Yes, of course.

PHILOSOPHER: What can one do to evade that responsibility? The answer is easy: Control the children. One allows the children to take only those paths that are safe and free from harm, without permitting any adventure. One keeps them under one's control as much as possible. One does not do this out of concern for the children. It is all for one's own self-protection.

YOUTH: Because one doesn't want to be held responsible for the children's failures?

PHILOSOPHER: That is how it goes. And this is precisely why people in positions in education and leaders charged with the management of organizations must always uphold the objective of self-reliance.

YOUTH: . . . So as not to get carried away with self-protection.

PHILOSOPHER: It is the same with counseling. When we give counseling, we are always very careful not to put the client in a position of "dependence" and "irresponsibility." Counseling that allows the client to say, "Thanks to you, I'm all better" is not solving anything. Because put another way, what they are really saying is: "I can't do anything by myself."

YOUTH: They are dependent on their counselors?

PHILOSOPHER: Right. And the same thing can be said about you—that is to say, about educators. Educators who let their students say things like, "Thanks to you, I was able to graduate," or "Thanks to you, I was able to pass my exams," are failing to provide education in the truest sense of the word. It is necessary to have the students gain the awareness that they can accomplish things on their own power.

YOUTH: But . . .

PHILOSOPHER: An educator is a lonely creature. One's students all finish school on their own power, and one isn't praised or appreciated for one's efforts. One does it without receiving gratitude.

YOUTH: So, one accepts that loneliness?

PHILOSOPHER: Yes. Rather than expecting gratitude from the students, one has the feeling that one has been able to contribute to the grand objective of "self-reliance." One finds happiness in the feeling of contribution. That is the only way.

YOUTH: . . . The feeling of contribution.

PHILOSOPHER: As I surely said to you three years ago, the essence of happiness is the "feeling of contribution." If you are hoping to receive gratitude from your students—if "It's thanks to you that . . ." are words you are waiting to hear—then please know that, in effect, you are standing in the way of their self-reliance.

YOUTH: Then, concretely speaking, in what way can one provide an education that does not put children in positions of dependence or irresponsibility? In what way can one aid in real self-reliance? You have to show me concrete examples, not concepts! Otherwise, I can't accept this!

PHILOSOPHER: All right. Suppose a child asks, "Can I go and play at my friend's place?" There are parents who will grant permission—"Of course you can . . ."—and then set the condition: ". . . once you've done your homework." And there are others who will simply prohibit their children from going out to play. Both are forms of conduct that put the child in a position of dependence and irresponsibility.

Instead, teach the child by saying, "That is something you can decide on your own." Teach that one's own life and one's everyday actions are things that one determines oneself. And if deciding things requires certain ingredients—knowledge and experience, for example—then provide them. That is how educators should be.

YOUTH: Decide on your own . . . Do they have that capacity for judgment?

PHILOSOPHER: If you doubt that, then you do not have enough respect for them yet. If you have real respect for them, then you should be able to let them decide everything on their own.

YOUTH: And what if that leads to an irreparable mistake!?

PHILOSOPHER: It is no different with paths that are chosen for them by their parents and by teachers. How can you say for sure that their choices will always end in failure, while the paths they are directed to will not?

YOUTH: But that's . . .

PHILOSOPHER: When children make mistakes, your responsibility is called into question. But that is not the kind of responsibility that one would stake one's life on. Responsibility, in the true sense of the word, is something that only that person can make themselves take. This is what has led to the idea of separation of tasks. The idea, in other words, that says, "Who ultimately is going to receive the end result brought about by the choice that is made?" You, who are not in the position of receiving the final responsibility, must not intervene in others' tasks.

YOUTH: You're saying to just leave the children alone?

PHILOSOPHER: No, I am not. I am saying to have regard for the children's decisions, and to help them in those decisions. And to convey to them that you are always ready to help them, and to watch over them at a distance from which you can help them that is not too close. Should those decisions end in failure, the children will learn from you the truth that "one can choose one's own life."

YOUTH: One can choose one's own life . . .

PHILOSOPHER: Heh-heh. "One can choose one's own life." This is the main overarching theme of our discussion today, so please be sure to remember it well. Yes, write it down in your notebook.

Now, let's take a little break at this juncture. Please reflect on the attitude you have taken when approaching your students.

YOUTH: No way, I don't need a break or anything! Let's keep at it!

PHILOSOPHER: The dialogue from this point onward is going to require even more concentration, which requires taking proper breaks. I'm going to make some coffee, so now would be a good time for you to calm down a bit and sort things out.

PART III

*From the Principle of Competition
to the Principle of Cooperation*

The objective of education is "self-reliance." And the educator is a "counselor." At the beginning, the youth had taken these two terms by their conventional definitions and had not given them much thought. As the discussion progressed, however, his doubts with regard to his own educational policy had grown rapidly. *Is my law-and-order-maintaining approach all wrong? Have I been fearing and standing in the way of my students' self-reliance? . . . No, there's no way . . . I've been supporting their self-reliance all along, there's no doubt about it.* The philosopher sitting before him silently stroked his fountain pen. *Look at him, so aloof and triumphant!* The youth wet his rough lips with coffee and began to speak in a tormented voice.

Negate Praise-Based Development

YOUTH: . . . The educator must not be a judge, but rather a counselor who is always there for the child. And rebuking is a form of conduct that only reveals one's own immaturity and gives rise to contempt. The final objective of education is self-reliance, and one must not stand in the way of that path. All right. For the time being, I will accept that one must not rebuke. But only if you acknowledge my next question.

PHILOSOPHER: Which is?

YOUTH: We often discuss with colleagues and parents whether "rebuke-based child-rearing" and "praise-based child-rearing" are right or wrong. It goes without saying that rebuke-based child-rearing is unpopular. This is likely due to the trends of our time, and there are many people who reject it from a moral standpoint. I agree with this standpoint myself, for the most part, as I have no desire to rebuke. On the other hand, praise-based child-rearing has an enormous following. Practically no one renounces it directly.

PHILOSOPHER: I suppose that is so.

YOUTH: However, Adler goes as far as to renounce praise. Three years ago, when I asked why, your answer went something like this: Praising is *the passing of judgment by a person of ability on a person of no ability*, and its goal is *manipulation*. And therefore, one must not praise.

PHILOSOPHER: Yes, I did say that.

YOUTH: I believed that, and I practiced "no-praising education" faithfully. However, this only lasted until my mistake was noticed by a certain student.

PHILOSOPHER: By a certain student?

YOUTH: It was several months ago. One of the worst problem children in our school handed in a book report he had written. It was an open assignment for summer vacation, and to my astonishment, he had gone and read Camus's *The Stranger.* Moreover, I was astonished by what he had written about the book! It was quite a wonderful essay, brimming with the fresh sensibilities that only a sensitive boy going through puberty could possess. Once I had read it, before I knew what I was doing, I praised him. I said, "Hey, great work! I had no idea you could write such a fine composition. It's changed my opinion of you!"

PHILOSOPHER: I see.

YOUTH: The moment I said it, I knew I'd messed up. Those words "it's changed my opinion of you," in particular, were filled with that judgment from above that Adler talks about. I guess you could say that I was belittling him.

PHILOSOPHER: Yes, because those words would not have come out otherwise.

YOUTH: Regardless, I had actually praised him. Moreover, I had done so with words of undisguised judgment. Now, what kind of expression do you think this problem child had on his face upon hearing those words? Was he repelled? . . . Ah, if only I could show you the face he made. He gave me such a smile, the likes of which he had never shown me before, the smile of a truly pure and innocent boy!

PHILOSOPHER: Heh-heh.

YOUTH: It felt just like my head had been in a fog, and now it was clearing before my eyes. And I said to myself, "What is up with Adler anyway? Thanks to getting caught up in this quackery, I've been giving an education that could only take away such a smile, such joyfulness. What kind of education is that!?"

PHILOSOPHER: . . . So, then you started praising?

YOUTH: Yes, of course. I praised without hesitation. Not only him, but the other students too. And when I did that, they seemed pleased with it, and they made progress with their schoolwork. The more I praised them, the more drive they exhibited. I could only think of it as a positive cycle of growth.

PHILOSOPHER: And you were getting excellent results.

YOUTH: Yes. But I wasn't just praising all of them indiscriminately, of course. I praised them according to their level of effort and success. Because if I did otherwise, the compliments would just be lies. That problem child who wrote the book report is a total bookworm now. He just reads tons of books and writes essays on them. It's really wonderful, isn't it, how books can open up one's world. I imagine that pretty soon the library room at school won't satisfy him anymore, and he'll start going to the university library. The library where I used to work!

PHILOSOPHER: If he does, that would be quite impressive.

YOUTH: I know. I'm sure you'll dismiss this. You'll say that it's a "demand for admiration," and the first stage of problem behavior. But, you know, the reality is completely different.

Even if his goal at the outset wasn't to receive praise, soon enough he would have discovered the joy of learning and the pleasure of accomplishment himself, and I'm sure he'll finish school and head out into the world on his own two feet. So, that leads to what Adler calls "self-reliance"!

PHILOSOPHER: Can you really say so for sure?

YOUTH: Please acknowledge this! Whatever you may think, due to the praising, the students regained their smiles and their ambition. This is an education I am giving with all the heat of my body and soul, to flesh-and-blood human beings living in the real world. In Adler's education, what warmth is there? What smiling faces?

PHILOSOPHER: Well, let's think about this together. Why do we stick to the principle of "one must not praise" in the education setting? There are children who enjoy and benefit from being praised, so why must one not praise? What are you risking by engaging in praise?

YOUTH: Heh-heh. I wonder what quibble you're coming up with next. Look, I'm not going to make any concessions here. If you're going to revise your arguments, now is the time.

Reward Gives Rise to Competition

PHILOSOPHER: Earlier, I brought up the subject of the classroom being a democratic nation. Do you remember?

YOUTH: Ha-ha, when you started calling people fascists? How could I forget?

PHILOSOPHER: Then I made the point that "an organization that is under the command of a dictator cannot escape corruption." When we think a little more deeply about why this is so, the reason "one must not praise" should become clear as well.

YOUTH: Do tell.

PHILOSOPHER: In a community that has a dictatorship in place instead of an established democracy, all rules regarding what is right and what is wrong are determined at the sole discretion of the leader. This is the case for nations, of course, and corporate entities as well. And it is the same with families and schools. The rules in such communities are applied in a quite arbitrary manner.

YOUTH: Ah, companies with top-down management and such are the epitome of that.

PHILOSOPHER: Now, though one might think that dictatorial leaders are despised by their "citizens," this is not always the case. Actually, there are probably more instances in which they enjoy their citizens' ardent support. Why do you think this is so?

YOUTH: Because the leader has some charismatic appeal?

PHILOSOPHER: No, that is not why. That is only a secondary, superficial reason. The main reason is the presence of a cutthroat system of reward and punishment.

YOUTH: Huh! How so?

PHILOSOPHER: One is severely punished for breaking rules and praised for obeying them. And one is recognized. In other words, the people are not actually obeying out of support for the leader's character or his thoughts and beliefs, but simply because they have the goal of "being praised" or "not being rebuked."

YOUTH: Well, sure. That's just how the world is.

PHILOSOPHER: Now, here is the problem: In that community where people gather with the goal of being praised, "competition" emerges. One finds it vexing when others are praised, and one is proud of being praised oneself. One is always concerned with how to be praised first and more frequently than everyone else—and beyond that, with how to have a monopoly on the leader's favor. In this way, the community comes to be controlled by a principle of competition for reward.

YOUTH: You're just beating around the bush. So you don't like competition, is that it?

PHILOSOPHER: Do you accept competition?

YOUTH: I accept it wholeheartedly. It seems to me that you are focusing only on the negative aspects of competition. Think of it more broadly. Whether it is in our schoolwork, in our arts and sports events, or in our economic activities once we enter society, it is due to the presence of our rivals keeping up the pace beside us that we continue to step up our efforts. The principle of competition lies at the very root of the power that pushes our society forward.

PHILOSOPHER: Is that so? When children are placed within the principle of competition and driven to contend with others, what do you think happens? . . . One's competitor is one's "enemy." Before long, the children start to adopt a lifestyle in which they believe that "all other people are my enemies" and "people are always looking for chances to trick me and must never be underestimated."

YOUTH: Why do you think so pessimistically? You have no idea the degree to which the existence of a rival acts as a stimulus for human growth. Nor the degree to which a rival can be a close friend one can rely on. I guess you've spent all your days absorbed in philosophy and lived a lonely life without close friends or rivals. Ha-ha, I'm starting to feel pity for you.

PHILOSOPHER: I accept wholeheartedly the value of having a sworn friend whom one may call a rival. However, there is no need whatsoever for one to compete with that rival, and one must not compete with him.

YOUTH: You accept rivals, but not competition? Oh my, you're contradicting yourself already!

The Disease of the Community

PHILOSOPHER: There is no contradiction or anything of the sort. Try to think of life as a kind of marathon. There are rivals running beside you. As this itself may act as a stimulus and feel reassuring, it does not present any problems. However, the moment one intends to "defeat" that rival, the situation changes completely.

The goal at the outset, which should have been "completing the race" or "running fast," transforms into the goal of "defeating that person." The rival, who should have been one's sworn friend, turns into an enemy who must be crushed. . . . And this brings out all manner of gamesmanship with regard to winning, and even results in interference and unfair conduct. Even after the race is over, one is unable to celebrate the victory of one's rival, and one struggles with feelings of envy and inferiority.

YOUTH: And that's why competition is unacceptable?

PHILOSOPHER: Wherever there is competition, gamesmanship and unfairness arise. There is no need to defeat someone. If one can complete the race, isn't that enough?

YOUTH: No way! You're naive if you have notions like that!

PHILOSOPHER: Then let's stop using this marathon example, and get back to real society. Unlike a marathon, in which people vie for the best time, in a community run by a dictatorial leader, there are no clear criteria for "winning." In a classroom, there are aspects besides schoolwork that can inform one's decisions. And as long as the judgment criteria are unclear, the world will be rampant with people who hold their comrades back, take credit for other people's work, and flatter their leaders so as to gain recognition only for themselves. You've witnessed this kind of thing even in your workplace, haven't you?

YOUTH: Uh, I guess so . . .

PHILOSOPHER: In order to prevent such situations from arising, an organization must implement a real democracy that is without reward and punishment, and without competition. Please consider that educating by trying to manipulate people with reward and punishment is an attitude that could not be any further removed from democracy.

YOUTH: Then tell me this. What do you think democracy is? What kind of organization or community would you call democratic?

PHILOSOPHER: A community that is run not on the basis of the principle of competition, but on the principle of cooperation.

YOUTH: The principle of cooperation!

PHILOSOPHER: Put cooperation with others above all else, instead of competition with others. If you can learn to run your classroom according to the principle of cooperation, your students are likely to adopt a lifestyle in which they see that "people are my comrades."

YOUTH: Ha-ha! Let's all get along and do our best? That sort of pipe dream doesn't hold water even in kindergartens today!

PHILOSOPHER: Suppose there is a student who has engaged repeatedly in problem behavior. Many educators would think to themselves, "What should I do about this student?" They would think about whether they should praise, rebuke, or ignore them, or if they should take some other approach. And then the student would be summoned to the teachers' room to be dealt with individually. But this way of thinking is wrong.

YOUTH: How so?

PHILOSOPHER: The problem here is the principle of competition pervading the entire classroom, not that the student got involved in problem behavior because they were "bad." If they had pneumonia, for example, it would not be that they are suffering from pneumonia as an individual, but that the entire classroom had a serious case of it from the outset. His problem behavior has appeared as one symptom of that. This is the way of thinking of Adlerian psychology.

YOUTH: A sickness of the entire classroom?

PHILOSOPHER: Yes, it is a disease called the principle of competition. What is needed of educators is to look at the community in which the problem behavior is occurring, not at the individual who is engaging in it. And then, instead of attempting to treat the individual, to go about treating the community itself.

YOUTH: How does one treat an entire classroom that has pneumonia!?

PHILOSOPHER: One stops engaging in reward and punishment, and continually nips competition in the bud. One rids the classroom of the principle of competition. That is the only way.

YOUTH: That would be impossible and have the opposite effect! Have you forgotten that I've already tried no-praising education and failed?

PHILOSOPHER: ... Yes, I know. At this point, let's step back for a moment and take stock of our discussion points. First of all, the strength- and rank-contesting principle of competition always results in "vertical relationships." Because it creates winners and losers, and the hierarchical relationships that exist between them.

YOUTH: Okay.

PHILOSOPHER: The "horizontal relationships" advocated by Adlerian psychology, on the other hand, are imbued with the principle of cooperation. One does not compete with anyone, and there is no winning or losing. It does not matter if there are differences in knowledge, experience, or ability between oneself and others. All people are equal, regardless of scholastic achievement or work performance, and it is in the very act of cooperating with others that building community has meaning.

YOUTH: So, this is what you are talking about when you refer to a democratic nation?

PHILOSOPHER: Yes. Adlerian psychology is a horizontal relationship–based "psychology of democracy."

Life Begins from Incompleteness

YOUTH: All right. The points of conflict are clear. You are saying that it is not a problem of the individual, but of the whole classroom. That the principle of competition permeating the classroom is the root of all evil.

I, on the other hand, focus on the individual. Why is that? Well, to borrow your words, it's respect. Each and every student, with their unique personality, exists as a splendid human being. There are all kinds of students: some quiet and well-behaved, some noisy and bright, some serious, and some with fiery temperaments. They are not a gathering without individual traits.

PHILOSOPHER: Of course, that's true.

YOUTH: But you, even as you talk about democracy, are trying not to look at each of the children individually, and instead view them only as a group. Moreover, you are preaching, "Everything will change if we change the system." That's more communist than anything else!

My view is different. It doesn't matter to me what the system is, democratic or communist or whatever. I deal with the pneumonia of each individual, not the pneumonia of the entire classroom.

PHILOSOPHER: Because that is what you have always done.

YOUTH: So, concretely speaking, how do you treat their pneumonia? This is another point of conflict. My answer is with approval. By fulfilling their need for approval.

PHILOSOPHER: Hmm.

YOUTH: I get it. I really get your denial of the need for approval. But I actively accept it. This conclusion is one I have arrived at based on firsthand experience, so it is not something I will concede easily. In their search for approval, these children are sick in the lungs and numb with cold.

PHILOSOPHER: Could you explain the reasoning behind your conclusion?

YOUTH: In Adlerian psychology, you deny the need for approval. Why is that? It is because as a result of their hopes of being accepted by another, a person under the sway of the need for approval will, before they know it, be living a life that conforms to that other person's wishes. In other words, they will be living another person's life.

But a person does not live to fulfill someone else's expectations. Whether that person is one's parent or one's teacher or someone else, one must not choose a way of living that fulfills "that person's" expectations. Do I have it right?

PHILOSOPHER: Yes.

YOUTH: Being constantly concerned about how one is judged by others, one can no longer live one's own life. It becomes a way of living that is no longer free. We have to be free. And if one hopes to find freedom, one must not seek approval. . . . This understanding is not mistaken, is it?

PHILOSOPHER: No, it is not mistaken.

YOUTH: It's a wonderful, truly courageous story. But you know, we can't be tough enough, unfortunately! Even you, if you were to observe the real everyday situation with the students, you'd understand. They put everything they've got into acting tough, but inside they're terribly insecure. They just don't seem to be able to get any confidence in themselves, and they suffer feelings of inferiority. They need approval from other people.

PHILOSOPHER: It's exactly as you say.

YOUTH: Don't agree so flippantly, you outdated Socrates! Look, the kind of people you're talking about are all just *David* statues!

PHILOSOPHER: *David* statues?

YOUTH: Yes, you know Michelangelo's statue of *David*, right? It's the ideal representation of the human body, all perfectly proportioned and muscular, without an ounce of flab to be found. But it's a supreme ideal image that is devoid of flesh and blood, not a human being that exists in reality. Real live people get stomachaches, and bleed! You are always talking about people as if they're that statue of *David* ideal!

PHILOSOPHER: Ha-ha, that's an interesting way of putting it.

YOUTH: What I am focusing on, however, is actual living people. I'm talking about sensitive, highly individualistic children who are awkward and thin-skinned in every way! I have to fulfill that need for approval for each one of them individually, and in a healthier manner. In a word, I have to praise them. If I don't, they won't be able to regain the "courage" they've lost!

You wear the mask of a man of virtue, but you keep the weak at arm's length. You've got idealistic theories of the heroic and the lionhearted, but nothing for real people!

PHILOSOPHER: I see. Though my words may have sounded like impractical, idealistic theories, that was not my intention. Philosophy must be an inquiry that is firmly grounded, with the awareness that the ideals we pursue are ideals. Let us take another angle to consider the reasons that Adlerian psychology does not accept the need for approval.

YOUTH: Huh. Trying to justify everything, just like Socrates!

PHILOSOPHER: The phrase you just brought up, "feelings of inferiority," is key.

YOUTH: Hmm. You want to talk about feelings of inferiority? Okay. I'm an expert on feelings of inferiority, you know.

PHILOSOPHER: First of all, during childhood, all humans without exception live with feelings of inferiority. This is a major premise of Adlerian psychology.

YOUTH: Without exception?

PHILOSOPHER: That's right. The human being is probably the only living thing with a body that takes longer to grow than the mind. While with other creatures, mind and body develop at the same speed, only in humans does development of the mind happen first while that of the body lags behind. In a sense, we are creatures who live bound hand and foot. Because though our minds are free, our bodies are not.

YOUTH: Hmm, that's an interesting viewpoint.

PHILOSOPHER: As a result, human children have to struggle with the gap between the "what I want to do" mental aspects and the "what I can do" physical aspects. There are things that the adults around them can do, but they cannot. That shelf where the adults put things is out of reach to them. Those stones the adults can carry, they cannot. And the subjects of their conversations are not things children can talk about.

. . . Children experience this sense of powerlessness, or one might say "incompleteness of self," and as a rule, cannot help but have feelings of inferiority.

YOUTH: So, they start their lives as "incomplete beings"?

PHILOSOPHER: Yes. Of course, children are not incomplete as people. It is only that the growth of their bodies has not caught up with that of their minds. But then the adults look only at their physical needs and start to "baby" them. They do not try to look at the children's minds. So it is only natural that the children suffer feelings of inferiority. Because even though their minds are no different from the adults' minds, their human worth is not being recognized.

YOUTH: All people start out as incomplete beings, so everyone experiences feelings of inferiority. That's a pretty pessimistic point of view.

PHILOSOPHER: It is not all bad. This feeling of inferiority, rather than being a handicap, has always been a stimulant of effort and growth.

YOUTH: Hmm, how so?

PHILOSOPHER: If human legs were as fast as horses', the horse-drawn carriage would never have been invented, and probably not the motor vehicle either. If we could fly like birds, the airplane would never have been invented. If we had fur like a polar bear, winter clothing would never have been invented, and if we could swim like dolphins, there would never have been a need for boats or marine compasses.

Civilization is a product of the need to compensate for the biological weakness of the human being, and the history of the human race is the history of its triumphing over its inferiority.

YOUTH: It's because we humans were weak that we were able to build up such a civilization?

PHILOSOPHER: That's right. And to extrapolate further, it is due to that weakness that humans create communities and live in relationships of cooperation. Ever since the hunter-gatherer age, we have lived in groups and cooperated with our comrades in hunting animals and raising children. It isn't that we wanted to cooperate with each other. It is that we were weak, so desperately weak, that we could not live separately.

YOUTH: It is due to that weakness that humans formed groups and built society. So, our power and our civilization are the fruits of our weakness.

PHILOSOPHER: Put the other way around, nothing is scarier to humans than isolation. Isolated people have not only their physical security threatened, but their mental security as well. Because instinctively, we are well aware that we cannot live alone. As a consequence, we are always longing for a strong "connection" with other people. . . . Do you understand what this fact means?

YOUTH: . . . No, what does it mean?

PHILOSOPHER: All people have community feeling inside them inherently. And it is something that is deeply linked to human identity.

YOUTH: Oh!

PHILOSOPHER: Just as one would not imagine a turtle without its shell or a giraffe with a short neck, there is no such thing as a human being who is completely cut off from other people. Community feeling is not something that is "attained," but something that one "digs up" from within oneself, which is why it can be shared as a feeling. As Adler elucidates, "Community feeling is always a reflection of the weakness of the body, and one from which we cannot be separated."

YOUTH: A community feeling resulting from human weakness . . .

PHILOSOPHER: Human beings are physically weak. But the human mind is second to none, much stronger than that of any other animal. I am sure you know well enough the degree to which spending one's days in competition with one's comrades is against the principles of nature. Community feeling is not some head-in-the-clouds ideal. It is a fundamental principle of life that resides within us humans.

Community feeling! That key concept of Adlerian psychology, which he had struggled so long to grasp and whose inner truth had been unfathomable, was now as clear as day to him. It is because of their physical weakness that humans create community and live in relationships of cooperation. Human beings always seek connection with other human beings. Community feeling exists inherently in everyone's minds. The philosopher was saying: *Dig up your own community feeling and seek connection with other people.* . . . With difficulty, the youth ventured a question.

The Courage to Be Myself

YOUTH: But . . . but why is the existence of that feeling of inferiority, and that community feeling, linked to not accepting the need for approval? Approving each other should actually strengthen the connection.

PHILOSOPHER: Well, at this point, it would behoove you to recall the five stages of problem behavior.

YOUTH: . . . Right. I have them written down here in my notebook.

PHILOSOPHER: What is the goal of the students' running about with their demand for admiration, and their launching into attention drawing and power struggles? Do you remember?

YOUTH: They want to be recognized, and they want to gain a special position within the classroom. That's right, isn't it?

PHILOSOPHER: Yes. Now, what is gaining a special position? Why do they seek to do that? What is your view on this?

YOUTH: I suppose it's because they want to be respected, to be viewed as superior, and that sort of thing.

PHILOSOPHER: Strictly speaking, no. In Adlerian psychology, a human being's most fundamental need is the "sense of belonging." In a word, we do not want to be isolated. We want to have the real feeling that "it's okay

135

to be here." Because isolation leads to social death, and eventually even to biological death. Now, how can they gain a sense of belonging?

. . . By gaining a special position within the community. By not becoming "everyone else."

YOUTH: By not becoming "everyone else"?

PHILOSOPHER: That's right. Their irreplaceable "this me" must not become "everyone else." They must secure a place to be that can be all their own at any time. They must not allow any wavering in their sense of belonging, that "it's okay to be here."

YOUTH: If that's the case, it proves my point even more. By praising them and fulfilling their earnest need for approval, one conveys to them, "You are not an incomplete being" and "You have worth." There's no other way!

PHILOSOPHER: You are wrong. Unfortunately, if they proceed in that direction, they will not be able to realize their true "worth."

YOUTH: Why is that?

PHILOSOPHER: There is no end to approval. So, they get praised and approved by others. As a result, they might find some fleeting realization of their own worth. Any joyful feeling thus gained, however, will be nothing more than something granted from outside them. They will be no different from clockwork dolls that do not move unless another person winds them up.

YOUTH: Uh . . . maybe so, but . . .

PHILOSOPHER: The person who is capable of feeling truly happy only upon being praised will seek to get praised more until the very last moment of their life. Such a person, having been left in a position of dependence, will lead a life of ceaseless seeking, a life without fulfillment.

YOUTH: Then what should one do?

PHILOSOPHER: Instead of seeking approval, one has to approve oneself, with one's own mind.

YOUTH: Approve oneself!?

PHILOSOPHER: Having another person decide the worth of "me"— that is dependence. Determining the worth of "me" oneself—that is self-reliance. If one were to ask which choice leads to a happy life, the answer should be clear. Your worth is not decided by someone else.

YOUTH: That's impossible! We don't have confidence in ourselves, and that's exactly why we need approval from others!

PHILOSOPHER: That is probably because we don't have enough "courage to be normal." It's okay to be just as we are. Your place to be is there, without needing to be a special being or be outstanding in any way. Let's accept our ordinary selves, ourselves as "everyone else."

YOUTH: . . . I am an ordinary "everyone else" without any outstanding qualities?

PHILOSOPHER: Aren't you?

YOUTH: Ha-ha. Making such insults comes perfectly naturally to you, doesn't it? That's the greatest insult I've ever received in my life.

PHILOSOPHER: It is not an insult. I am a normal person. And "being normal" is an aspect of individuality. It is nothing to be ashamed about.

YOUTH: Enough of your wisecracking, you sadist! What person today would not take being told "You are a common, ordinary human being" as an insult? What person would be comforted by hearing "That's individuality too," and take you seriously!?

PHILOSOPHER: If you feel insulted by these words, you are probably still trying to be a "special me." Consequently, you seek approval from others. And therefore you seek to gain admiration and draw attention, and continue to live within the framework of problem behavior.

YOUTH: Stop it! Stop messing around!

PHILOSOPHER: Look, instead of placing worth on "being different from other people," place worth on "being yourself." That is true individuality. A way of living in which, instead of being yourself, you compare yourself to others and try to accentuate only your difference, is just a way of living in which you deceive both others and yourself.

YOUTH: You're saying, rather than laying emphasis on my difference from others, place worth on being myself, even if that's mediocre . . . ?

PHILOSOPHER: Yes. Because your individuality is not something relative—it is absolute.

YOUTH: . . . Well, let's talk about the conclusion I have arrived at with regard to this individuality and such. It is a conclusion that would seem to indicate the limitations of school education.

PHILOSOPHER: Hmm. I would like to hear about it.

That Problem Behavior
Is Directed at "You"

YOUTH: . . . I have been uncertain all along whether I should say this or not, but here we are. It's time to come clean. Somewhere inside me, I am feeling that school education has limitations.

PHILOSOPHER: Limitations?

YOUTH: That's right. For us educators, there is a limit to what can be done.

PHILOSOPHER: What do you mean?

YOUTH: In the classroom, there are bright and extroverted students, and there are modest, inconspicuous students too. To use Adler's terminology, everyone has their particular lifestyle, or worldview. No one is the same. That's individuality, right?

PHILOSOPHER: Yes.

YOUTH: Then where do they get those lifestyles from? Without question, it is from their families.

PHILOSOPHER: Indeed. The influence of the family is quite strong.

YOUTH: The students spend the better part of each day at home. And they share "everyday life itself" with their families in impossibly close quarters, under a single roof. Some parents are passionate about education, and some are passive when it comes to child-rearing. Many households have divorced or separated parents, or have lost a parent. There are differences in economic status, of course, and there are also parents who abuse their children.

PHILOSOPHER: Yes, unfortunately there are.

YOUTH: On the other side of things, the period of time that we teachers can commit to each student is the scant few years until they graduate. Compared to the parents, who can give almost a lifetime of commitment, the preconditions differ too greatly.

PHILOSOPHER: And what do you conclude from that?

YOUTH: First of all, the kind of "broadly defined education" that would include personality formation is the responsibility of the family. In other words, in the case of a violent problem child, it is the parents who must assume the unequivocal responsibility of having raised such a child. There can be no mistaking this to be the responsibility of the school. Therefore, the role that is expected of us teachers is one of "narrowly defined education"; that is to say, education on the level of curriculum. We cannot get any more involved than that. I feel quite ashamed about this conclusion, but it is the reality.

PHILOSOPHER: I see. Adler would probably reject this conclusion out of hand.

YOUTH: Why? How!?

PHILOSOPHER: Because, it must be said, the conclusion you have drawn disregards the personalities of the children.

YOUTH: It disregards their personalities?

PHILOSOPHER: In Adlerian psychology, we regard all manner of human words and actions in terms of interpersonal relationships. For example, when we have a person who has been engaging in wrist-cutting or other self-harm, we do not regard that conduct as being directed at nothing at all. The act of self-harm is directed at someone—just as we saw with the revenge problem behavior. In other words, we think that for all words and actions, there is "another party" at whom they are directed.

YOUTH: And then?

PHILOSOPHER: How do the students in your charge behave within their families, on the other hand? This is something that we cannot know.

It is doubtful that they have exactly the same face that they do at school, however. Because whether it's the face they show their parents, the face they show their teachers, the face they show their friends, or the face they show their junior and senior schoolmates, no one wears the same face all the time.

YOUTH: Well, maybe so.

PHILOSOPHER: And now there is a student in your classroom who is repeatedly engaging in problem behavior. At whom is that problem behavior directed? At "you," of course.

YOUTH: What . . . !?

PHILOSOPHER: When that student puts on the mask of the face they show you, they are repeatedly engaging in problem behavior directed at "you" and no one else. It is not the parents' problem. It is a problem that has arisen entirely within the relationship between you and the student.

YOUTH: Are you saying that their education at home doesn't matter?

PHILOSOPHER: We cannot know about that, and we cannot intervene. Regardless, right now they are facing you and resolving something to the effect of, "I'm going to disrupt this teacher's class" or "I'll disregard the homework this teacher assigns me." Of course, there are cases in which the student is continuing to engage in problem behavior at school, and at the same time resolving, "I'll be a good child in front of my parents." As this is behavior that is directed at you, you have to take it in, first of all.

YOUTH: It's a task that I have to solve in my class!?

PHILOSOPHER: You've got it exactly. Because they are seeking help from "you" and no one else.

YOUTH: Those kids keep on engaging in problem behavior directed only at "me" . . .

PHILOSOPHER: Moreover, they're doing it right in front of you. And choosing times when it will be within your field of vision. They are looking for a place to be, in another "world" that is not their home, that is to say, in your classroom. Through respect, you have to show them that place to be.

Why a Person Wants to
Become a Savior

YOUTH: . . . Adler is utterly terrifying! If I hadn't learned about Adler, I wouldn't need to be struggling like this. I would have guided my students without a doubt in my head, yelling at the ones who should be rebuked and issuing high praise to the ones who should be praised, just as the other teachers do. The students would have been grateful to me, and I would have been able to fulfill the role of teaching as my vocation. More than ever, I wish I had never heard about all these ideals!

PHILOSOPHER: It is true that once one learns of Adler's way of thinking, there is no turning back. There are many people who have been exposed to Adler who, just like you, try to brush it off by saying, "That's an idealistic theory" or "It's unscientific." And yet, they can't give up on it. Somewhere inside them, there is a feeling of incongruity that remains. They cannot help but be aware of their "lie." Truly, one might call it a strong medicine of life.

YOUTH: Let's sort out the points of discussion up until now. First of all, one must not rebuke children. Because rebuking is conduct that damages each other's respect. And anger and reprimand are low-cost, immature, and violent means of communication. Do I have it right?

PHILOSOPHER: Yes.

YOUTH: And again, one must not praise either. Praising gives rise to the principle of competition within the community, and implants in the child a lifestyle, or worldview, of "other people are my enemies."

PHILOSOPHER: That's right.

YOUTH: Furthermore, rebuking and praising—in other words, reward and punishment—stand in the way of the child's self-reliance. Because reward and punishment are a conduct of trying to keep the child under one's control, and the adult who relies on this conduct is, somewhere deep inside, afraid of the child's self-reliance.

PHILOSOPHER: They want the child to stay a child forever. Consequently, they use that reward and punishment to restrain children. Prepared with such excuses as "I'm doing it for you" or "It's because I'm worried about you," they try to make the child stay a child. . . . This sort of attitude in adults contains no respect whatsoever and cannot lead to the building of good relationships.

YOUTH: That's not all. Adler denies even the need for approval. He says that we should not seek approval from others, but instead switch to approval of ourselves.

PHILOSOPHER: Yes. This is a problem that should be considered within the context of self-reliance.

YOUTH: I know. Self-reliance is one's own determining of one's worth. The attitude of the need for approval, of trying to get another person to decide one's worth, is just dependence. That is what you're saying, right?

PHILOSOPHER: Yes. Some people, on hearing the term "self-reliance," will only be able to consider its economic aspects. But there are ten-year-old children who are self-reliant. And there are people in their fifties and sixties who are not. Self-reliance is a matter of the psyche.

YOUTH: ... All right. It certainly is a wonderful logic. As a philosophy presented here in this study at least, it is completely beyond reproach.

PHILOSOPHER: But you are not satisfied with this philosophy.

YOUTH: ... Ha-ha, you're right, I'm not. If it stops at philosophy, and cannot be brought down to a practical scientific level that will hold water outside the walls of this study, and in my classroom in particular, then I won't be able to agree with it.

You are the one who got me into Adler. Of course, making the final decision is my job. But if you're only going to lay out the prohibitions—"one must not do this" and "one must not do that," and so on—without indicating some other choice, I'll be at a loss for what to do. As things stand, I can't go back to reward-and-punishment education, and I'm not ready to put complete faith in Adler's education either!

PHILOSOPHER: The answer is probably a simple one.

YOUTH: Sure, maybe it's simple for you. Because all you can say is "Believe in Adler, choose Adler."

PHILOSOPHER: No. Whether or not you give up on Adler doesn't matter at this point. The most important thing to do now is to move away from the subject of education for the time being.

YOUTH: Move away from education!

PHILOSOPHER: I am telling you this as a friend. You have been talking about education all day long, but that is not where your real troubles lie. You have not learned to be happy yet. You are not able to have the "courage to be happy." And you did not choose the path of the educator because you wanted to save children. You wanted to be saved through the act of saving them.

YOUTH: What did you say!?

PHILOSOPHER: By saving another person, one tries to be saved oneself. By passing oneself off as a kind of savior, one attempts to realize one's own worth. This is one form of the superiority complex that people who cannot dispel their feelings of inferiority often fall into, and is generally referred to as a "messiah complex." It is a mental perversion of wanting to be a messiah, a savior of others.

YOUTH: Don't mess around!! What are you suggesting, all of a sudden!?

PHILOSOPHER: Raising one's voice in anger in such a way is also an expression of feelings of inferiority. When one's feelings of inferiority are aroused, one tries to resolve them by using the emotion of anger.

YOUTH: Argh, you . . . !!

PHILOSOPHER: The important thing is what we will get into next. Salvation by a person who is unhappy does not overcome self-satisfaction and does not make anyone happy. While you set about saving children, you are actually still in the midst of unhappiness yourself. You are hoping only to realize your own worth. And if that is the case, there is no point in bouncing around more education theory. Find happiness on your own, first of all. Otherwise, any discussion we engage in here is likely to end in a fruitless exchange of invective.

YOUTH: Fruitless? This discussion will be fruitless!?

PHILOSOPHER: If you are going to choose "to not change" things as they are, I will respect that decision. It is fine to return to school just as you are now. But if you are going to choose "to change," then today is the only day to do so.

YOUTH: . . .

PHILOSOPHER: This is something that goes beyond work or education, and is about questioning your life itself.

M̲ove away from the discussion of education. You don't want to save the children—you're just stuck in a vortex of unhappiness and want to save yourself through education. . . . To the youth, these words amounted to a "letter of recommendation to resign" that negated his entire being as an educator. *I had my eyes opened to Adler's shining light and set my heart on the path of education in the face of all manner of hardship, and this is the treatment that was waiting for me!?* And then a thought occurred to him. . . . *I wonder if this is how the people of Athens felt when they informed Socrates that he was sentenced to death. This man is too dangerous. If he's left to his own nefarious devices, the poison of his nihilism will spread across the world.*

Education Is Friendship, Not Work

YOUTH: ... Ah, you've got to be thankful for my self-control. If it were ten or even five years ago, I wouldn't have had the self-control for this, and I probably would have smashed my fist into your nose by now.

PHILOSOPHER: Heh-heh, well, that wouldn't be good. But I see your point. Adler himself experienced violence from his clients on occasion.

YOUTH: I'll bet he did! It's just rewards for pushing such extreme views!

PHILOSOPHER: One of Adler's patients for a time was a girl who suffered from severe mental illness. This was a girl who had been struggling with symptoms for eight years already, and two years prior to their meeting, it had been deemed necessary to commit her to an institution. Of their first encounter, Adler states, "She barked like a dog, spat, tore at her clothes, and tried to eat her handkerchief."

YOUTH: ... That is beyond the scope of counseling.

PHILOSOPHER: Yes. Her symptoms were so serious that her doctor had given up on her case. So the doctor reached out to Adler to see if he couldn't do anything to help her.

YOUTH: And did he?

PHILOSOPHER: He did. In the end, she recovered completely, and managed to return to society, earn her own living, and live in harmony with those around her. As Adler relates, "No one who sees her now would believe that she had ever suffered from insanity."

YOUTH: What sort of magic did he use?

PHILOSOPHER: There is no magic to Adlerian psychology. Adler only spoke to her. He spoke to her for eight days in a row, but she did not utter a word. He continued her counseling, and after thirty days she began to talk in a confused and unintelligible way.

Adler understood the reason why she behaved like a dog to be as follows: She felt that she had been "treated like a dog" by her mother. He did not know whether or not she really had been treated that way. But at the very least, she did feel that way. And as an act of rebellion against her mother, she had resolved subconsciously to "really play the role of dog."

YOUTH: As a kind of self-harm, as it were?

PHILOSOPHER: Exactly—it was self-harm. Her dignity as a human being had been hurt, and she was keeping the wound open with her own hands. That is why Adler was speaking to her patiently, as an equal human being.

YOUTH: . . . I see.

PHILOSOPHER: Now, after he had continued her counseling in this way for some time, one day she began hitting him all of a sudden. What did Adler do then? . . . He put up no resistance whatsoever and allowed her to hit him. When, carried away by the impulse, the girl then broke a window and cut her hand on the glass, Adler quietly bandaged the wound.

YOUTH: Huh, it's like an episode straight out of the Bible, isn't it!? You're trying to make Adler out to be some kind of a saint. Ha-ha! Sorry, but I'm not so easily fooled!

PHILOSOPHER: Adler was not a saint, of course, and neither was he choosing the path of nonresistance from a moral viewpoint in this case.

YOUTH: Then why didn't he put up any resistance?

PHILOSOPHER: Adler explains that when the girl first began to speak, he had the feeling "I am her friend." And when she began attacking him for no reason, he simply "let her hit me and looked friendly." In other words, Adler did not interact with the girl as part of his job or his profession, but as a friend.

Say a friend of yours, who has been mentally ill for a long time, suddenly became confused and started hitting you. . . . If you can imagine such a scene, then maybe you can see that Adler's actions were not in any way out of the ordinary.

YOUTH: . . . Well, I can understand if the person is truly a friend.

PHILOSOPHER: Now. There is something we need to recall again, at this point. The statement: "Counseling is reeducation for self-reliance, and the counselor is an educator." And further, the definition: "The educator is a counselor."

Adler, who was both a counselor and an educator, would interact with each client as a friend. So, you too should interact with each of your students as a friend. Because you, too, are an educator and a counselor.

YOUTH: Huh!?

PHILOSOPHER: The reason you have failed at Adlerian-style teaching and are still unable to find real happiness is a simple one. It is that you have been avoiding the three "life tasks" of work, friendship, and love.

YOUTH: The life tasks!?

PHILOSOPHER: You trying to face your students is "work" now. But as Adler shows from his own experience, your relationship with the students is one of "friendship." You started off on the wrong foot, and if you don't do something about it, there's no way your teaching is going to go over well.

YOUTH: You're talking nonsense! Behave like I'm a friend to those kids?

PHILOSOPHER: One does not "behave" as if that is so. One builds a relationship of friendship, in the truest sense of the word.

YOUTH: You're wrong! I am proud to be a professional educator. It is precisely because I am a professional, and that it is work for which I receive remuneration, that I am able to bear the great responsibility!

PHILOSOPHER: I understand what you want to say. But my view remains the same. The relationship you should create with your students is one of friendship.

Three years ago, we did not manage to discuss the life tasks deeply enough. Once you understand the life tasks, I think you should be able to grasp the meaning of the phrase I began with today: "the biggest choice in life." And the meaning of "the courage to be happy," as well.

YOUTH: And what if I'm not convinced?

PHILOSOPHER: Then you should just give up on Adler, and give up on me too.

YOUTH: ... It's funny. You're really sure of yourself, aren't you?

PART IV

Give, and It Shall Be
Given Unto You

There was no clock in the philosopher's study. How long had they been engaged in this discussion? How many more hours were left until daybreak? Even as he reproached himself for having forgotten his watch, the youth ruminated over the content of their discussion until now. . . . *A messiah complex? Build a "friendship" relationship with my students? This is no joke! You say that I misunderstand Adler, but you misunderstand me! And you're the one who's avoiding your life tasks, and avoiding contact with other people, by shutting yourself up in this study of yours!*

All Joy Is Interpersonal
Relationship Joy

YOUTH: I am in the midst of unhappiness now. I am troubled, not about school education, but only about my own life. And the reason for that is that I am avoiding my "life tasks." . . . That's what you're telling me, right?

PHILOSOPHER: If you are going to sum it up in a few words, yes.

YOUTH: Moreover, you are saying that instead of facing my students as my "work," I need to build "friendship" relationships with them. Because, in other words, that's what Adler did. Adler faced his clients as friends. That Adler did it, so I should do the same. . . . Do you think I could find such a reason convincing?

PHILOSOPHER: If my stance were that you should do something simply because Adler did, I very much doubt you would find it convincing. The basis for my argument lies elsewhere entirely.

YOUTH: If you don't reveal what that is, it will be nothing more than pretext.

PHILOSOPHER: All right. Adler called the tasks an individual must confront in order to live in society the "life tasks."

YOUTH: I know. The task of work, the task of friendship, and the task of love, right?

PHILOSOPHER: Yes. The important point here is that these are tasks of interpersonal relationships. In a "work task" situation, for example, rather than treating one's labor itself as the task, one focuses on the interpersonal relationships that are associated with it. In that sense, it may be easier to understand the tasks by thinking of them as "work relationships," "friend relationships," and "love relationships."

YOUTH: So, in other words, focus on the "relationships," not on the "actions."

PHILOSOPHER: Right. Now, why does Adler focus on interpersonal relationships? This is an aspect that lies at the very core of Adlerian psychology. Do you know the answer?

YOUTH: I suppose it's his premise that "all problems are interpersonal relationship problems"; that is to say, his definition of "suffering."

PHILOSOPHER: That's right. But this definition itself requires some explanation. In the first place, what reason could he have to assert that "all problems are interpersonal relationship problems"? Adler says . . .

YOUTH: Ah, get to the point! I'll explain it succinctly, so we'll be done with it. "All problems are interpersonal relationship problems." To get to the true meaning of this statement, you just consider the opposite.

Supposing there were only one "me" existing in the universe, what would it be like? It would most likely be a world in which neither language nor logic existed. There would be no competition, no envy, and no loneliness either. Because it is only with the existence of "another person who shuns me" that a human being can feel loneliness. Loneliness cannot arise if one is truly alone.

PHILOSOPHER: Yes, loneliness exists only within relationships.

YOUTH: But the fact is that such a hypothesis is impossible. Because in principle, there is no way that we can live separated from other people. Every person is born from a mother's womb and raised on her milk. We are born in a condition of not being able to turn over in bed on our own, let alone feed ourselves.

And then, the moment when we, as babies, open our eyes and confirm the existence of another person—in most cases, that would be the mother—"society" comes into being. With the appearance of the father, siblings, and others from outside the family, society becomes increasingly complex.

PHILOSOPHER: Yes.

YOUTH: The birth of society is, in other words, the birth of "suffering." In society, we are exposed to all manner of suffering, such as conflict, competition, envy, and loneliness, not to mention feelings of inferiority. Between "me" and "that person," there is a resounding dissonance. Never again can we return to those days of tranquility, when we were enveloped in warm amniotic fluid. We have no choice but to live in the incessant hubbub of human society.

If other people did not exist, no problems would exist either. But there is absolutely no way that we can escape the existence of other people. Therefore, all the problems that people have are interpersonal relationship problems. . . . Is there anything incorrect in this understanding?

PHILOSOPHER: No, you have done an excellent job of summing things up. But allow me to add one point. If all problems stem from interpersonal relationships, is it all right to just sever one's relations with other people? Is it all right to just stay away from other people, and shut oneself up in one's room?

No, it is not all right. It is not all right at all. The reason it is not is that all the joy of humanity comes from interpersonal relationships too. A person living "all alone in the universe" would have to lead a life that is utterly flat and featureless, with neither problems nor joy.

Concealed beneath the statement put forth by Adler, "All problems are interpersonal relationship problems," there lies this definition of happiness: "All joy is interpersonal relationship joy."

YOUTH: Which is precisely why we must confront our life tasks.

PHILOSOPHER: Yes, it is.

YOUTH: All right. Now, about that question. Why do I have to build friendship relationships with my students?

PHILOSOPHER: Right. What is "friendship," in the first place? Why are we assigned the task of friendship? Let's use Adler's words as our guide. Adler makes the following statement with regard to friendship: "In friendship, we see with the eyes of another, listen with the ears of another, and feel with the heart of another."

YOUTH: That's what you mentioned earlier as . . .

PHILOSOPHER: Yes, it is the definition of "community feeling."

YOUTH: What are you saying? That we learn human knowledge and gain community feeling through friendship relationships?

PHILOSOPHER: No, the word "gain" is incorrect. Earlier, I spoke of community feeling as a feeling that resides within all people. It is not something one strives to gain, but something one digs up from within oneself. So, to be precise, it is a feeling that we "dig up through friendship."

It is in our friendship relationships that our contribution to others is tested. A person who does not embark on friendship can never hope to find a place to be within the community.

YOUTH: Hold on a minute!

PHILOSOPHER: No, I will continue until the conclusion. The point of concern here is this: Where does one put friendship into practice? . . . I am sure you already know the answer. The place where children first learn friendship and begin to dig up community feeling. That place is school.

YOUTH: Hey, hold on, I said! You're developing things too fast, and I don't get what's what anymore! If school is the place where children learn friendship, I should become their friend?

PHILOSOPHER: This is a point that is misunderstood by many people. The relationship of "friendship" is not something limited to the relationship between friends. Friendship relationships are often formed even when relations are not such that one would call the other person a friend. So, what is this thing that Adler speaks of as "friendship"? Why does it connect to community feeling? Let's go into this in depth.

Do You Trust? Do You Have Confidence?

YOUTH: Let me make sure I understand this again. You are not telling me to be friends with those kids. Have I got it right?

PHILOSOPHER: Yes. Three years ago, on that last day when everything was covered with a blanket of white snow, I explained the difference between "trust" and "confidence." Do you remember?

YOUTH: Trust and confidence? You just keep changing the subject. Yes, of course, I remember that, and I've always kept it in mind. It was a fascinating insight.

PHILOSOPHER: Now, let's go back over it again, in your words. How would you explain "trust"?

YOUTH: All right. Simply put, "trust" is believing in the other party with conditions. For example, when one borrows money from a bank. It goes without saying that the bank will not lend you money unconditionally. They will ask for some kind of collateral, such as real estate or a guarantor, and give you a loan that corresponds to the value of that. And they'll slap on the interest too. This is an attitude of "we'll lend to you because we believe in the value of the collateral you've given us," not one of "we'll lend to you because we believe in *you*." In other words, they are not believing in "that person," they are believing in the "conditions" of that person.

PHILOSOPHER: What about "confidence"?

162

YOUTH: It is doing without any set conditions whatsoever when believing in others. Even though one might not have sufficient grounds for believing, one believes. One believes unconditionally without concerning oneself with such things as collateral. That is "confidence." Instead of believing in the "conditions" of that person, one believes in "that person." You could even say that one focuses not on material worth, but on human worth.

PHILOSOPHER: I see.

YOUTH: Furthermore, if I may supplement this explanation with my own interpretation, it is also to believe in "oneself who believes in that person." Because how can one ask for anything like collateral if one does not have confidence in one's own judgment? It is a confidence in others that cannot exist without self-confidence.

PHILOSOPHER: Thank you very much. You've summed it up wonderfully.

YOUTH: . . . I'm a pretty good student, aren't I? Look, I spent a long time following Adler, and I gleaned a lot from his writings. And most important, I have put his ideas into practice in an educational setting. So I am not rejecting Adler in an emotional way without a basis of understanding.

PHILOSOPHER: Of course you are not. But please do not misunderstand me here. You are neither my disciple nor my student.

YOUTH: . . . Ha-ha!! So, insolent fellows like me aren't your disciples, is that it? What a masterpiece this is. I'm getting an Adler advocate angry.

PHILOSOPHER: It is clear that you are a lover of wisdom. Without shying away from doubt, or from thinking with your own words, you move forward to attain higher understanding. In other words, you are a lover of wisdom, a philosopher. And I am not a person who confers teachings from above. I am nothing more than a wisdom-loving philosopher on the same level as you.

Youth: You're a philosopher, without a teacher or disciples, who is my equal? Then it's possible that you could recognize your errors and adopt my views?

Philosopher: Of course it is. I hope to learn many things from you. In fact, there are fresh discoveries each time we talk.

Youth: Huh. Just because you're flattering me doesn't mean I'm going to let up on the criticism. Now, why did you bring up trust and confidence?

Philosopher: The life tasks of work, friendship, and love that Adler upholds are delineated by the distance and depth of our interpersonal relationships.

Youth: Yes. You explained that before.

Philosopher: Even so, though one can say "distance" and "depth" in a single breath, these are things that are hard to grasp. There are many aspects that you have probably misunderstood. Please think about it in a simple manner, like this: the difference between work and friendship is "Is it trust or is it confidence?"

Youth: Trust or confidence?

Philosopher: Right. Work relationships are relationships of "trust," and friend relationships are relationships of "confidence."

Youth: What do you mean?

Philosopher: Work relationships are condition-based relationships that involve either some vested interest, or external factors—cooperating with someone because we happen to be at the same company, for example. Or there's a person whose personality you don't like, but he's someone you do business with, so you maintain and promote the relationship. But you have no intention of maintaining that relationship away from work. This is truly a relationship of "trust" that is formed as a result of the vested interest that is your work. Regardless of your individual preferences, you have to form that relationship.

On the other hand, in friendship, there is no "reason to befriend this person." It is not a vested interest, and neither is it a relationship that is compelled by external factors. It is purely a relationship formed out of the intrinsic motivation that "I like this person." To borrow the phrase you used earlier, one is believing in "that person," not in the "conditions" of that person. Clearly, friendship is a relationship of "confidence."

YOUTH: Ah, it's getting tiresome again. If that's the case, why did Adler use such words as "work" and "friendship"? He could've just discussed interpersonal relationships in terms of "trust," "confidence," and "love" from the start. You're just complicating things and trying to blow smoke!

PHILOSOPHER: All right. I will explain as simply as possible the reason that Adler chose the word "work."

The youth was sure of it. *Adler probably regards poverty as a virtue, and economic activity in general as something vulgar. That's why he can disparage work and say things like "Build friend relationships with your students." What a joke.* The youth was just as proud to be a career professional as he was to be an educator. *It is precisely because we engage in education as a profession, and not out of enjoyment or charity, that we are able to responsibly execute our professional duties.*

His coffee cup had been empty for a long time, and the night was far advanced. Nevertheless, the youth's eyes shone with burning intensity.

Why Work Becomes a Life Task

YOUTH: Let me ask you this: In the first place, what was Adler's opinion with regard to work? Did he look down on work, or on the earning of money through work? You know, if Adlerian psychology, with its tendency toward empty idealism, is to become a true, grounded theory, this is a discussion that is absolutely necessary.

PHILOSOPHER: To Adler, the meaning of engaging in work was simple. Work is a means of production for staying alive in our earth's harsh natural environments. That is to say, he thought of work as a task quite directly linked to survival.

YOUTH: Hmm. Well, that's rather banal. It's just, "Work so that you can eat"?

PHILOSOPHER: Yes. When we think of surviving, of eking out a living, the fact that we humans must engage in some kind of labor is a self-evident truth. On that basis, Adler focused on the paradigm of the interpersonal relationship that establishes "work."

YOUTH: What do you mean?

PHILOSOPHER: In the absence of sharp teeth, wings for soaring the skies, or sturdy shells, the human being in the natural world is basically physically inferior to all other animals. That is why we have chosen to live in groups and learned to protect ourselves from outside enemies. In groups, we have lived and raised our children while hunting, engaging in agriculture, securing our food supply, and maintaining our physical security. . . . The answer that Adler derived from this is embodied in a brilliant few words.

YOUTH: What conclusion did he come to?

PHILOSOPHER: We humans did not just herd together. Humans discovered the revolutionary way of working called "division of labor." Division of labor is the incomparable survival strategy that the human race acquired in order to compensate for its physical inferiority. . . . This is Adler's final conclusion.

YOUTH: . . . Division of labor!

PHILOSOPHER: If we only herded together, that would be no different from what most animals do. But humans herded together on the basis of an advanced system of division of labor. Or one could say that we created society in order to divide up the labor. To Adler, the "work tasks" were not mere tasks of labor. They were "tasks of the division of labor" that were premised on our connection with others.

YOUTH: So, it is because of its premise on our connection with others that "work" is a task of interpersonal relationships?

PHILOSOPHER: That's right. Why do humans work? In order to survive and stay alive in the harsh natural world. Why do humans create society? In order to work and divide up the labor. Living, working, and building society are all inseparable.

YOUTH: . . . Hmmm.

PHILOSOPHER: Before Adler, the division of labor was explored by others, such as Adam Smith, who pointed out its significance from the standpoint of economics. Adler, however, was likely the first to recognize the division of labor in the field of psychology. Moreover, it was he who saw its significance as the paradigm of interpersonal relationships. It is thanks to this key concept that the meaning of labor to humans, and the meaning of society, have become clear.

YOUTH: . . . Ah, this is an extremely important matter. Please go into a bit more detail.

PHILOSOPHER: Adler's inquiries always start with the same major points. To quote Adler, "Perhaps if we lived on another planet which gave everything easily and bountifully, working would not be a virtue. Perhaps it would be a vice and being lazy would be a virtue."

YOUTH: He says some funny things! . . . And then?

PHILOSOPHER: But there is no such environment on our planet. Our food supply is limited, and no one is going to provide us with dwelling places. So, what do we do? . . . We work. And we do not work alone, but with our comrades. In conclusion, Adler states, "The answer that is logical and in accord with common sense is that we should work, cooperate, and contribute."

YOUTH: That's a thoroughly logical conclusion.

PHILOSOPHER: The important thing here is that Adler is not stipulating that labor itself is "right." Regardless of moral right and wrong, we have no choice but to work, and no choice but to engage in the division of labor. We have no choice but to build relationships with others.

YOUTH: So, I guess it's a conclusion that goes beyond morality.

PHILOSOPHER: In other words, human beings cannot live alone. It is not that we cannot bear loneliness or that we want people to talk to, so much as simply not being able to live, on the level of survival. And in order to "divide labor" with another person, one must believe in that person. One cannot cooperate with someone whom one doubts.

YOUTH: That is a relationship of trust?

PHILOSOPHER: Yes. Human beings do not have the choice of "not believing" in each other. It would be impossible for us to not cooperate and not divide up the labor. A relationship, not of cooperating because one likes that person, but of having to cooperate whether one likes it or not. You can think of it that way.

YOUTH: Fascinating! No, I mean it, this is wonderful! . . . I'm finally getting the work relationship. Division of labor is necessary for living, and mutual trust is necessary in order to carry it out. And there is no alternative. We cannot live alone, and not trusting is not an option. We have no choice but to build relationships. . . . That's how it is, right?

PHILOSOPHER: Yes. It truly is a life task.

All Professions Are Honorable

YOUTH: Well, let's really get to the heart of the matter. A relationship in which there is no alternative but trust, a relationship in which there is no alternative but to cooperate. This is something that goes beyond the actual setting where labor take place, isn't it?

PHILOSOPHER: Yes, it is. I suppose the most easily understood example would be the typical division-of-labor relationships among teammates at sports competitions and the like. In order to win a match, they have no choice but to cooperate regardless of their individual likes and dislikes. It is not an option to ignore someone because one doesn't like them, or to sit out a game because one can't get along with one's teammates, or anything like that. You forget "liking" and "not liking" the moment the match begins. You treat your teammate not as a "friend," but as one of the "functions" of the team. And you yourself try to excel as one of those functions.

YOUTH: . . . Ability is given precedence over good relations.

PHILOSOPHER: Such aspects are probably unavoidable. So much so, that Adam Smith himself declares "self-interest" to lie at the very foundation of division of labor.

YOUTH: Self-interest?

PHILOSOPHER: Suppose there's a man who is an expert at making bows and arrows. If you use the bows and arrows he makes, your rate of accuracy will improve drastically, and your ability to kill or wound will be enhanced as well. The thing is, he's not an expert at hunting. He is slow on his feet, has weak eyesight, and is just not good at hunting, even with his own excellent bows and arrows. ... And then, one day, it occurs to him: "I'll devote my time to making bows and arrows."

YOUTH: Huh. Why?

PHILOSOPHER: If he devotes his time to making bows and arrows, he should be able to make a few dozen of them per day. If he distributes them to comrades who are good at hunting, they will probably shoot down more game than they ever have before. Later, he can get his share of the game they bring back home. That is the choice that allows for the maximization of profit for both parties.

YOUTH: I see—so it's not just working together, it's everyone being in charge of their own field of expertise.

PHILOSOPHER: From the hunting experts' point of view, there would be nothing better than getting their hands on some highly accurate bows and arrows. They won't have to make the bows and arrows themselves, and they'll be able to concentrate on hunting. And then they'll divvy up the game they catch with everyone. ... In this way, they will perfect a more advanced division-of-labor system that is one step beyond "going hunting in a group."

YOUTH: That's certainly rational.

PHILOSOPHER: The important thing here is that no one is sacrificing themselves. That is to say, the combination of pure self-interest is establishing the division of labor. As a result of everyone having pursued self-interest, a fixed economic order is created. This is the division of labor that was devised by Adam Smith.

YOUTH: In a division-of-labor society, if we follow "self-interest" all the way, ultimately it connects to "other-interest."

PHILOSOPHER: That's right.

YOUTH: But Adler is recommending "contribution to others," isn't he? Three years ago, you asserted this point quite forcefully. That the aim to contribute to others is a grand compass of life, a guiding star. Doesn't the idea of giving precedence to one's own profit contradict "contribution to others"?

PHILOSOPHER: It does not contradict it at all. First, one embarks on work relationships. One is tied to other people and to society by interest. And so, it is only upon having pursued self-interestedness that one finds "contribution to others."

YOUTH: Even so, if one is engaged in role-sharing, surely superiority and inferiority will arise there, won't they? Say there's one person who has an important job, and another who has a job that doesn't really matter. Doesn't this deviate from the principle of equality?

PHILOSOPHER: No, it does not deviate from it at all. Viewed from the standpoint of the division of labor, all professions are honorable. Whether prime minister, business owner, farmer, factory worker, or the oft-ignored profession of housewife, all work is "something that has to be done by someone in the community," and all of us are just doing our share of that work.

YOUTH: So, all forms of work are of equal value?

Philosopher: Yes. To paraphrase Adler with regard to the division of labor, "A person's worth is decided by the way in which they fulfill their role in assigning the division of labor in their community."

In other words, a person's worth is not something that is decided by what kind of work they engage in. It is decided by *the attitude* with which they undertake that work.

Youth: The attitude with which they undertake it?

Philosopher: For example, you quit your job as a librarian and chose the path of an educator. Today, you have dozens of students in front of you, and you truly feel that you have been entrusted with their lives. You feel that you have a really big job that is useful to society. Perhaps you even think that education is everything, and that other professions are insignificant in comparison.

But when one considers the community as a whole, the librarian's work, the middle school teacher's work, and all other work is "something that has to be done by someone in the community," and no superior or inferior can exist there. If anyone is going to be superior or inferior, it will only be in the attitude with which they undertake that work.

Youth: What is "the attitude with which they undertake the work," in such a case?

Philosopher: In principle, each person's "ability" is treated as important within the division-of-labor relationship. When it comes to company employment, for example, the level of ability becomes a criterion. There is no denying this. However, after starting the division of labor, ability alone is insufficient for character evaluation, or for judging how relationships should be. Rather, the question "Do I want to work with this person?" becomes important. Because if it does not, it will become difficult to help each other.

The major factor in deciding "Do I want to work with this person?" or "Do I want to help when this person is having a hard time?" is that person's integrity, and the attitude with which they undertake work.

YOUTH: Okay, so if one undertakes it with integrity and sincerity, there is no difference in worth between the person who performs lifesaving work and the person who takes advantage of others' weaknesses and engages in usurious lending?

PHILOSOPHER: No, there is no difference.

YOUTH: Huh!

PHILOSOPHER: Our community has all manner of work available, and the presence of people there who engage in each kind of work is crucial. That diversity itself is abundance. If the work is one that has no value, it will not be needed by anyone, and will be done away with. If it has not been done away with and is still surviving, it must possess some value.

YOUTH: Does that mean that even usurious lending has value?

PHILOSOPHER: It is natural that one might think so. The most dangerous thing is to uphold a mediocre "justice" that declares what is good and what is bad. A person who is drunk on justice will be unable to recognize anyone else's values and will end up crusading for the "intervention of justice." What lies ahead with such intervention is a society of uniform grayness that is robbed of freedom. You can do whatever kind of work you like, and it does not matter what kind of work other people do either.

The Important Thing Is "What Use One Makes of That Equipment"

YOUTH: . . . Interesting. This thing you're calling the Adlerian "division of labor" is certainly an interesting concept. The human being in the natural world is much too weak to live alone. That is why we formed groups and came up with the way of working called "division of labor." When we carry out the division of labor, we can bring down a mammoth, and we can farm and build dwellings.

PHILOSOPHER: That's right.

YOUTH: And the division of labor begins by trusting others, regardless of one's likes and dislikes. We cannot live if we don't divide up the labor. We cannot live if we don't cooperate with other people, which is another way of saying that we cannot live without trusting others. This is the division-of-labor relationship, and the "work" relationship.

PHILOSOPHER: Yes. Take the rules of traffic on public roads, for example. It is on the basis of our trust that "all people follow the rules of traffic," that we pass through a green light. We are not having confidence in people unconditionally. We do look to the left and right first. But even then, we are placing a certain trust in other people whom we have never met. In a sense, this too is a work relationship, in that it is fulfilling a shared interest in the smooth flow of traffic.

YOUTH: I see. I guess that works. At this point, I can't find anything about the division of labor that needs to be refuted. But have you forgotten? The departure point of this discussion was your remark that I should "build friend relationships" with my students.

PHILOSOPHER: No, I have not forgotten.

YOUTH: But, considered in the context of the division of labor, your argument makes less sense than ever. Why on earth would I enter into friend relationships with my students? Clearly, it's a work relationship, isn't it? Neither I nor my students have any memory of having chosen each other. It's just a relationship that was mechanically assigned between people who were originally complete strangers. We have no choice but to cooperate, though, in order to run the classroom and fulfill the objective of graduation. It is truly a work relationship that is entered into with a common interest.

PHILOSOPHER: I think it is only natural to have such doubts. Now, let's go over each of the points we have discussed today. What is the objective of education? What is the work that is required of the educator? Our discussion began with these questions.

Adler's conclusion is a simple one. The objective of education is self-reliance, and the work that is required of the educator is assistance toward self-reliance. I believe that you agreed with this point.

YOUTH: Yes, I'll allow it, in any case.

PHILOSOPHER: Then in what way can one assist children to gain self-reliance? In response to this doubt, I spoke about "starting from respect."

YOUTH: Indeed, you did.

PHILOSOPHER: Why respect? What is it? Here, we must recall the words of Erich Fromm. Namely, that respect is "the ability to see a person as [they are]," and "the placing of worth on that person being that person."

YOUTH: Of course, I remember.

PHILOSOPHER: Have regard for the person as they are. You are fine just as "you." There is no need to be special. There is value in you just being "you." Through respect, and by conveying that, the children will regain the "courage" they had lost and begin climbing the steps of self-reliance.

YOUTH: Yes, that's our discussion in a nutshell.

PHILOSOPHER: Now, this is the definition of respect that has emerged here: "to have regard for the person as they are." Is it "trust" that lies at the very root of respect, or is it "confidence"?

YOUTH: Huh?

PHILOSOPHER: One has regard for "that person" as they are, without imposing one's own system of values. The reason one can do such a thing is that one is accepting and believing that person unconditionally. In other words, one is having confidence in them.

YOUTH: Respect and confidence are synonymous?

PHILOSOPHER: One could say that. Put the other way around, one cannot have confidence in someone whom one does not respect. Whether or not one can have confidence in someone depends on whether or not one respects that person.

YOUTH: Ah, I get it. The gateway to education is respect. And respect is confidence. Therefore, a relationship based on confidence is a friend relationship. It's that sort of syllogism, right?

PHILOSOPHER: That's right. One would not be able to respect one's students in a trust-based work relationship. And that is exactly how it is for you now.

YOUTH: ... No. No, that is not where the issue lies. I can place unconditional confidence in my best friend, for example. I can accept him as the person he is. It is possible enough in such a case.

The issue is not the "act" of having confidence, but the "target." You are telling me to build friend relationships with all my students, and to have unconditional confidence in all my students. Do you think that such a thing is really possible?

PHILOSOPHER: Of course I do.

YOUTH: How!?

PHILOSOPHER: Suppose, for example, a person who is critical of everyone around them, saying, "I don't like this thing about so-and-so," and "This aspect of that person is unbearable," and such. And then they lament over it: "Ah, I'm so unlucky. I'm not blessed when it comes to meeting people."

Are such people really not blessed when it comes to meeting people? No. Absolutely not. It is not that they are not blessed with comrades. It is only that they have not tried to make comrades, or in other words, that they have not tried to embark on interpersonal relationships.

YOUTH: ... So, one can become a comrade to anyone?

PHILOSOPHER: One can. Maybe the relationship between you and your students is one of all of you, due to accidental factors, just happening to be in that place. Maybe until that time, you were all total strangers who didn't even know each other's faces or names. And maybe you won't become what you call best friends.

But remember that statement of Adler's: "The important thing is not what one is born with, but what use one makes of that equipment." Regardless of who the other person is, one can give them respect, and one can believe in them. Because that is something that is the product of one's single-minded resolve and is not affected by the environment or the target.

YOUTH: So, it's that again? You're returning to the problem of courage? You're saying it's the courage to believe!

PHILOSOPHER: Yes. Everything comes back to that.

YOUTH: No, it doesn't! You don't know about real friendship!

PHILOSOPHER: What do you mean?

YOUTH: You don't have true close friends, and you don't know about real friendship, and that's why you can talk about such pipe dreams! I'll bet you've never had anything but shallow associations with people. That's why you can say that anyone will do! You're the one who's been running away from interpersonal relationships, and from your life tasks!!

In the natural world, the human being is such a small and feeble creature. To make up for that weakness, humans created society and brought forth "division of labor." Division of labor is an incomparable survival strategy that is unique to the human race. . . . This was the "division of labor" conveyed by Adler. If the discussion had ended there, the youth would have applauded Adler enthusiastically. But when it came to the "friendship" that the philosopher began presenting next, he was far from convinced. *This guy can talk about such a well-grounded division of labor, and then in the next breath change the subject to friendship, and start espousing ideals after all! And now he brings up "courage" again!*

How Many Close Friends
Do You Have?

PHILOSOPHER: So, you have a best friend, don't you?

YOUTH: I don't know how he feels about it. But I do have one friend in whom I have what you call "unconditional confidence."

PHILOSOPHER: What kind of person is he?

YOUTH: He was my classmate at university. The guy wanted to become a novelist, and I was always the first to read his work. Late at night, when everyone else was sound asleep, he'd show up out of the blue at the boardinghouse where I lived and say, his voice shaking with excitement, "Read this short story I just completed!" or "Hey, I found this amazing passage in a Dostoyevsky novel!" Even now, he still sends me new pieces of writing every time he finishes them, and when I got hired as an instructor, he celebrated with me.

PHILOSOPHER: Was this fellow a close friend of yours from the start?

YOUTH: How could he have been!? Friendship is something that takes time to cultivate. He didn't become a close friend overnight. We laughed together, marveled at things together, and it grew into an ever so slightly complicit relationship. We cultivated the friendship gradually and became close friends, while also going through some intense conflicts at times.

PHILOSOPHER: So, in other words, at some point he was elevated from being a friend to being a "close friend"? Was there something that led to your thinking of him as a close friend?

YOUTH: Hmm, I wonder. If I had to, I guess I'd say it was when I felt sure that "with this guy, it'll be okay to talk frankly about everything."

PHILOSOPHER: You cannot talk frankly about everything with a normal friend?

YOUTH: That's how it is for everyone. All people go through life wearing a "social mask." People go through life hiding their true feelings. Even with a friend you exchange smiles and jokes each time you meet, you never get to see his real face. We choose our subjects of conversation, our attitudes, and our words. All of us interact with our friends while wearing a social mask.

PHILOSOPHER: Why can't you take off the mask when you are with a normal friend?

YOUTH: Because if I did such a thing, the relationship would fall apart! You can talk all you want about "the courage to be disliked" and such, but there's no such thing as a person who would actually wish to be disliked. We wear the mask to prevent needless conflict from arising, and to prevent the relationship from falling apart. If we don't do that, society won't operate.

PHILOSOPHER: To put it more directly, are we avoiding being hurt?

YOUTH: ... Yes, I'll acknowledge that. Certainly, I don't want to get hurt, and I don't want to hurt someone else. But you see, it isn't only out of self-protection that we wear the mask. It's actually more out of kindness! If we were to live only with our real faces and our true feelings, we would hurt too many people. Just imagine what the world would be like if everyone were crashing their true feelings into each other. . . . It's a perfect picture of hell, with blood spattered all around!

PHILOSOPHER: But you can take off the mask when you are with your close friend, and even if that leads to you hurting each other, the relationship won't fall apart, will it?

YOUTH: Sure, I can take it off, and the relationship won't fall apart. Even if he commits a faux pas once or twice, I don't think that would be reason enough to sever my relationship with him. Because the relationship is based on accepting each other's strengths and shortcomings.

PHILOSOPHER: That is a wonderful relationship.

YOUTH: And the important thing is there are precious few people in the world who will allow us to have such a sense of certainty. One would be lucky to find even five during one's lifetime. . . . Well, please get to my question. Do you have any true close friends? Because from the way you talk, you really sound like a person who doesn't know anything about close friends or about friendship, and only has comrades he knows from books and daydreams.

PHILOSOPHER: Yes, of course, I have several close friends. And to borrow your words, they are people with whom I can have my "real face," or even if they "commit a faux pas once or twice, I don't think that would be reason enough to sever my relationship."

YOUTH: Huh, what kind of people are they? School friends? Comrades in philosophy or in Adlerian research?

PHILOSOPHER: For example, you.

YOUTH: Huh!? What did you say?

PHILOSOPHER: As I have said before, to me, you are an irreplaceable friend. I have never worn a mask in your presence.

YOUTH: So, does that mean that you have "unconditional confidence" in me!?

PHILOSOPHER: Of course I do. If I did not, this dialogue would not be able to take place.

YOUTH: . . . No way!

PHILOSOPHER: It's the truth.

YOUTH: This isn't a joke! You think you can get away with manipulating a person's heart this way, you phony wise man!! I'm not the kind of person who's taken in by such honeyed words!

First, Believe

PHILOSOPHER: Why are you so adamant in your denial of "confidence"?

YOUTH: But it's the other way around! I wish you'd tell me: What is the point in believing in a complete stranger, and in believing in them without conditions? To believe in someone unconditionally is to be unquestioning of others, and to believe in them blindly. It's the same as saying one should just become an obedient sheep!

PHILOSOPHER: You are wrong. Believing is not just swallowing everything one hears, hook, line, and sinker. One is skeptical with regard to that person's thoughts and beliefs, and to the statements he makes. One steps back for a moment and thinks for oneself. There is nothing wrong with doing so, and it is important work. On top of that, even if someone is telling lies, one must believe in the whole person who lies to us.

YOUTH: ... Huh!?

PHILOSOPHER: Believe in others. This is not the passive conduct of swallowing something hook, line, and sinker. Real confidence is in all respects an active approach.

YOUTH: What are you saying?

PHILOSOPHER: For example, I would like as many people as possible to learn of Adler's ideas. I hope to present Adler's words. However, this wish is not something that can be realized through my labor alone. It is something that forms upon there being a "will to listen" on the part of the person who receives my words, and on the part of the person who listens deeply to them.

Then, in what way can I get someone to receive and listen deeply to my words? I cannot force them and say, "Believe in me." That person is free to believe or not to believe. The only thing I can do is believe in the other party to whom I am speaking. That is all.

YOUTH: Believe in the other party?

PHILOSOPHER: Yes. If I were to speak to you about Adler with a sense of distrust, it'd just go in one ear and out the other. Regardless of the validity of my discourse, you would have no intention of listening from the very start. That would be perfectly natural.

But I want you to believe in "me." I want you to believe in me and listen to Adler's words. So, I will believe in you first. Even if you yourself are trying not to believe.

YOUTH: You want me to believe in you, so you believe in me first . . . ?

PHILOSOPHER: Right. Take, for example, when parents who do not have confidence in their children are worrying about various things. Even if their arguments are quite reasonable ones, they do not reach the children. Actually, the more reasonable the arguments are, the more the children want to oppose them. Why do they oppose them? Because their parents don't actually see them at all, and even as they're in the midst of distrusting themselves, they're getting all the standard lectures.

YOUTH: . . . Reasonable arguments not being understood as such is something I am well aware of on a daily basis.

PHILOSOPHER: We try not to believe only in the words of "a person who will believe in me." We do not judge the other party by the "rightness of their opinion."

YOUTH: I'll accept that that aspect exists, but the rightness of your opinion is going to be questioned in the end!

PHILOSOPHER: All conflicts, from a small quarrel to a war between nations, arise as a result of collisions of "my justice." "Justice" is something that takes on all manner of forms depending on the era, the environment, or individual standpoints, and no matter where one may go, there is never only one justice, or one solution. It would seem that it is dangerous to overestimate "rightness."

Within that, we are looking to find common ground. We are looking for a connection with other people. We are hoping to join hands. . . . If you want to join hands with others, you have to reach out with your hands too.

YOUTH: No, that's another arrogant notion! Why? Because when you say you "believe" in me, what you're thinking is, *So, believe in me, too*, right?

PHILOSOPHER: No, I am not. It is not something one can force. I believe in you, whether you believe in me or not. I keep on believing. That is the meaning of "unconditional."

YOUTH: How about right now? I do not believe in you. Even after being so firmly rejected and verbally abused with cruel words, can you still completely believe in me?

PHILOSOPHER: Of course I can. I believe in you just as I did three years ago. If I did not, we would not be able to engage in discussion for such a long time, and with such earnestness. A person who does not believe in others cannot engage in direct discussion. Such a person would not think, *With this guy, it'll be okay to talk frankly about everything,* as you so admirably put it.

YOUTH: . . . Argh, this is impossible! There is no way I can believe such words!

PHILOSOPHER: That is fine. I will just go on believing. I will believe in you, and I will believe in human beings.

YOUTH: Oh, shut up! So, you're a religious type now!?

People Never Understand Each Other

PHILOSOPHER: I have said this before, but I am not a follower of any particular religion. However, in both Christianity and Buddhism, in such ways of thought that have been cultivated and refined over a period of several thousand years, there is a power that cannot be ignored. It is because they contain uniform truths that they have not been done away with, and still survive today. . . . For example, do you know the "love thy neighbor" phrase from the Bible?

YOUTH: Yes, of course. It's that neighborly love that you enjoy talking about so much.

PHILOSOPHER: This phrase is in circulation with an important part left out. In the Gospel of Luke, in the New Testament of the Bible, it says, "Love thy neighbor as thyself."

YOUTH: As thyself . . . ?

PHILOSOPHER: That's right. He is saying not just to love one's neighbor, but to love them as much as one loves oneself. If one cannot love oneself, one cannot love others. If one cannot believe in oneself, one cannot believe in others. Please think of the phrase as carrying that connotation. You are insisting that you "cannot believe in other people," but that is because you have not managed to truly believe in yourself.

YOUTH: You're making too many assumptions!

PHILOSOPHER: Being self-centered does not mean looking only at oneself because one "likes oneself." In actuality, the opposite is the case, and it is because one is unable to accept oneself as one is, and because one is constantly beset with anxiety, that one has concern only for oneself.

YOUTH: So, you're saying that because I "hate myself," I look only at myself!?

PHILOSOPHER: Yes, that's right.

YOUTH: . . . Oh, what an unpleasant psychology!

PHILOSOPHER: It is the same with regard to other people. For example, when recalling a lover one had a bad breakup with, for a while it's only the bad things about the other person that come to mind. This is evidence that you want to feel, "I'm glad we broke up," and that some uncertainty remains about your decision. If you don't tell yourself, "I'm glad we broke up," you might lose your resolve. See it as being that kind of stage.

And if you recall the good points about a former lover, that means you do not have the need to actively dislike that person and can be free from feelings toward that person. . . . Either way, the issue is not whether "one likes or dislikes the other person," but whether "one likes oneself now."

YOUTH: Hmm.

PHILOSOPHER: You have not yet learned to like yourself. As a result, you cannot believe in others, you cannot believe in your students, and you are unable to embark on friend relationships.

That is exactly why you are now trying to gain a sense of belonging through your work. You are trying to prove your worth by being successful in your work.

YOUTH: What is wrong with that? Recognition at work is recognition from society!

PHILOSOPHER: No. In principle, we may say that it is your "functions" that are recognized as a result of your work, not "you." If someone who possesses greater functions appears, the people around you will turn to that person. That is the principle of the marketplace, the principle of competition. As a result of that, you will never be able to get out of the vortex of competition, and never gain a true sense of belonging.

YOUTH: Then how can one gain a true sense of belonging?

PHILOSOPHER: One has confidence in other people, and one embarks on friend relationships. That is the only way. We cannot gain happiness solely by dedicating ourselves to our work.

YOUTH: But ... even if I believe in someone, there's no way to know if that person will have confidence in me, or if that person will embark on a friend relationship with me!

PHILOSOPHER: This is the separation of tasks. How that other person feels about you, and what sort of attitude they take toward you, are the other person's tasks and are not something you have any control over.

YOUTH: No way, that doesn't make sense. Because if we are going to treat the separation of tasks as a prerequisite, wouldn't that mean that we never really know each other?

PHILOSOPHER: It is a given that it is not possible to know everything that the other party is thinking. One believes in another person as an "unknowable being." That is confidence. We humans are beings who cannot know each other, and that is exactly why believing is the only way.

YOUTH: Hah! So everything you're saying is religion after all!!

PHILOSOPHER: Adler was a thinker who had the courage to believe in human beings. Actually, given the situation he was placed in, maybe he had no choice but to believe.

YOUTH: What do you mean?

PHILOSOPHER: This is the perfect opportunity for us to take a look back at the circumstances that led Adler to put forward his concept of community feeling. Why, in the face of criticism, did Adler advance this idea? Naturally, he had a substantial reason.

Life Is Made Up of Trials of "Nothing Days"

PHILOSOPHER: After parting ways with Freud, in 1913, the year before the outbreak of World War I, Adler named his psychological approach "individual psychology." One might say that Adlerian psychology, at its inception, was drawn into the war.

YOUTH: Did Adler serve in the war?

PHILOSOPHER: Yes, he did. When World War I began, Adler, who was forty-four at the time, was conscripted as a medical officer and served in the department of neurology and psychology at a military hospital. His job as a medical officer was one and one only: to provide treatment to the soldiers in his care, and to return them to the front lines as soon as possible.

YOUTH: . . . Huh, to return them to the front. Well, the purpose of giving them treatment is pretty clear!

PHILOSOPHER: You're quite right. The soldiers he treated were sent back to the front, and without that treatment there was no way they would ever have been able to return to society. For Adler, who as a child had lost a younger brother and had dreamed of becoming a doctor, the duties of a medical officer must have been distressing in the extreme. Later, Adler said of his time as a medical officer, "I felt throughout the war as a prisoner feels."

YOUTH: I can barely imagine how difficult a role it must have been for him.

PHILOSOPHER: World War I, which was begun as the "war to end all wars," progressed into an unprecedented all-out war that devastated Europe and involved even noncombatants. It goes without saying that this tragedy had a great effect on Adler and other psychologists of his time.

YOUTH: Concretely speaking, how?

PHILOSOPHER: Freud, for example, after the experience of the war, proposed the existence of the "death drive," which would become known as "Thanatos" or "destrudo." This is a concept that has been subjected to all manner of interpretation, but it may be best understood as the "destructive impulse with regard to life."

YOUTH: Without considering the existence of such an impulse, there would be no way to explain the tragedies unfolding before them.

PHILOSOPHER: I suppose that is how it was. On the other hand, what Adler, who had experienced the same war directly from the standpoint of a medical officer, proposed was "community feeling," which was quite the opposite of Freud. I would say that this is a particularly noteworthy point.

YOUTH: Why did he bring up community feeling at that time?

PHILOSOPHER: Adler was in all respects a practical person. One might say that he did not focus on war or murder, or the "causes" of violence, in the way that Freud did, but considered instead, "In what way can we put a stop to war?"

Are we beings who long for war, for murder and violence? Surely not. If we can nurture community feeling—that is to say, the awareness that all people must have of regarding other people as comrades—we can prevent conflict. And furthermore, we have the power to accomplish that. ... Adler believed in people.

YOUTH: . . . In his pursuit of such empty ideals, however, he was criticized as unscientific.

PHILOSOPHER: Yes, he received a great deal of criticism, and lost many comrades. Adler was not unscientific, however. He was constructive. His principle was "not what one is born with, but what use one makes of that equipment."

YOUTH: But wars are still occurring all over the world.

PHILOSOPHER: To be sure, Adler's ideals have yet to be realized. One wonders if they are actually realizable. Regardless, progressing toward those ideals is something that we can do. Just as a human being can always continue to grow as an individual, the entire human race should be able to continue growing. We must not use the unhappiness of our current situation as a reason for abandoning our ideals.

YOUTH: So, if we don't abandon our ideals, someday there will be no more war?

PHILOSOPHER: Mother Teresa, on being asked, "What can one do to promote world peace?" gave the following reply: "Go home and love your family." It is the same with Adler's community feeling. Instead of doing something for world peace, just have confidence in the person in front of you. Become comrades with that person in front of you. That daily, small accumulation of confidence will someday get rid of even conflict between nations.

YOUTH: All you need to think about is what's right in front of you!?

PHILOSOPHER: For better or for worse, that is the only place we can start from. If one wants to rid the world of conflict, one has to free oneself of conflict first. If you wish your students would believe in you, you need to believe in your students first. Instead of engaging in the whole story while leaving oneself out of it, one takes the first step as a part of the whole.

YOUTH: . . . You spoke of this three years ago. "You should start."

PHILOSOPHER: Yes. "Someone has to start. Other people might not be cooperative, but that is not connected to you. My advice is this: You should start. With no regard to whether others are cooperative or not." This was Adler's answer to a question regarding the actual effectiveness of community feeling.

YOUTH: Will my first step change the world?

PHILOSOPHER: Maybe it will change, and maybe it will not. But one does not need to think now about what the results will be, or anything like that. What you can do is have confidence in the people closest to you. That is all.

Our trials and decisions as human beings do not come only with such symbolic life events as taking university entrance examinations, gaining employment, or getting married. For us, it is our "nothing days" that are our trial, and it is in everyday life "here and now" that the big decisions must be made. People who manage to get by and avoid those trials are unlikely to ever attain real happiness.

YOUTH: Hmm.

PHILOSOPHER: Before arguing over the state of the world, have some thought for your neighbor. Have some thought for your interpersonal relationships on "nothing days." That is all we can do.

YOUTH: . . . Ha-ha. So you mean, "Love thy neighbor as thyself."

Give, and It Shall Be Given Unto You

PHILOSOPHER: It seems there are still some points that you find unconvincing.

YOUTH: Unfortunately, there are quite a few. As you so aptly put it, my students do look down on me, but they aren't the only ones who do that. Almost nobody out there acknowledges that I have some worth, and they just ignore my existence.

If they had regard for me and would listen to what I say, my attitude would probably change. And maybe it would even be possible to have confidence in them. But the reality is different. Those guys think little of me, and they always have.

If there is one thing that can be done in such a situation, it is this: to have my worth acknowledged through my work. That is all. Confidence and respect and such—all that comes later!

PHILOSOPHER: So, in other words, other people should have regard for one first, and then one becomes successful in one's work in order to gain the respect of others?

YOUTH: That's right.

PHILOSOPHER: I see. Well, think of it this way. Having unconditional confidence in other people, having respect for them, is a "giving" conduct.

YOUTH: Giving?

PHILOSOPHER: Yes. It should be easy to understand if we use money as an example instead. Basically, it is people in a position of affluence who can engage in "giving" something to others. If one does not have enough saved up, one cannot engage in giving.

YOUTH: Okay, when it comes to money, that makes sense.

PHILOSOPHER: And now, you are seeking only "to have something given" to you, without having given anything. Just like a beggar. It is not that you are poor financially, but that you are poor in spirit.

YOUTH: You disrespectful son of a . . . !!

PHILOSOPHER: We have to keep our hearts abundant and give what we have saved up to others. We must not wait for respect from other people, but must ourselves have respect and confidence in them. . . . We must not become poor-spirited.

YOUTH: An objective like that isn't philosophy, and it isn't psychology either!

PHILOSOPHER: Heh-heh. Then let's take it even further, and bring in a quote from the Bible. Are you familiar with the phrase "Ask, and it shall be given you"?

YOUTH: Yes. At least, it's a phrase I've heard on occasion.

PHILOSOPHER: Adler would probably put it like this: "Give, and it shall be given unto you."

YOUTH: . . . Wow!!

PHILOSOPHER: It is because of one's giving that one is given to. One must not wait to have something given to one. One must not become a beggar of the spirit. . . . This is an extremely important viewpoint when considering one other interpersonal relationship, continuing from "work" and "friendship."

YOUTH: That one other, in terms of . . .

PHILOSOPHER: At the beginning today, I said the following: Everything we are discussing may be summarized by "love." There is no task that is stricter or more difficult, or more testing of courage, than the love that Adler speaks of. At the same time, however, the stairway to understanding Adler may be found by embarking on love. Actually, it is no exaggeration to say that that is the only way.

YOUTH: The stairway to understanding Adler . . .

PHILOSOPHER: Do you have the courage to climb it?

YOUTH: There is no way I can answer that unless you show me that stairway, or whatever it is. After that, I will decide whether to climb it or not.

PHILOSOPHER: All right. Then let's turn our attention to "love," which is the final gateway in our life tasks, and is also the stairway to understanding the ideas of Adler.

PART V
Choose a Life You Love

The youth had to admit it was true. At the very beginning of the evening's discussion, the philosopher had informed him: All the issues you are experiencing now may be summarized in the discussion of "love." They had spent many hours talking together, and at long last, they had arrived at the issue of love. *What is there to talk about with this man concerning love anyway? What do I even know about love in the first place?* Looking down, he found his notebook now filled with what appeared to be notes, written in a scrawl that he could barely make out himself. Feeling slightly unsure of himself, and finding the silence unbearable, the youth let out a laugh.

Love Is Not Something One "Falls" Into

YOUTH: Heh-heh. Still, it's kind of funny.

PHILOSOPHER: What is?

YOUTH: I can't help but laugh, you know. Two scruffy guys putting their heads together in this small study and trying to talk about love. In the middle of the night, no less!

PHILOSOPHER: Come to think of it, I suppose it is an unusual situation.

YOUTH: So, what will we talk about now? Maybe we should hear the story of your first love? The ruddy-faced young philosopher in love, what will become of him! . . . Ha-ha, it sounds interesting.

PHILOSOPHER: . . . Direct talk of romance and love brings about embarrassment. You are young, and I know well that desire to be facetious to cover it up. You are not the only one who does so. Many people fall silent when confronted by love and pass it off with lifeless generalizations. As a result, almost all the love that gets talked about does not quite grasp its actual state.

YOUTH: It's easy for you, huh? So, tell me, what's this "lifeless generalization" about love?

PHILOSOPHER: For example, the lofty love that is unforgiving of defilement, and deifies the other person. Or conversely, the animal love of succumbing to sexual drives. Or further, the biological love of intending to transmit one's genes to a new generation. Most representations of love in the world revolve around one of these types.

To be sure, we can demonstrate a certain understanding of all these kinds of love. We can accept that there are such aspects. At the same time, however, we should be aware that something is missing. Because all we hear about is conceptual "divine love" and instinctive "animal love," and no one even attempts to speak of "human love."

YOUTH: . . . A "human love" that is neither divine nor animal.

PHILOSOPHER: Now, why does no one try to come to grips with human love? Why is it that people do not attempt to discuss real love? What is your view on this?

YOUTH: Well, I guess you're right about feeling embarrassed when it comes to talking about love. Because it's the private thing that one wants to keep concealed most of all. If it's the kind of love for humanity that is steeped in religion, people are only too happy to talk about it. In a sense, it's someone else's affairs, and it's nothing more than impracticable theory anyway. But it's not so easy to speak about one's own love.

PHILOSOPHER: Because it is about an inextricably involved "me"?

YOUTH: Yes. It's something that feels as embarrassing as it would be to take off one's clothes and run around naked. And there's another reason as well. The moment of falling for someone is almost entirely the result of the action of the subconscious. So, no matter what, it is a bit of a stretch to explain it using logical language.

. . . I suppose it's the same as the audience member who is moved on seeing a play or a movie and cannot explain why they are crying. Because if the tears were so rational as to be explainable with words, they wouldn't flow in the first place.

PHILOSOPHER: I see. Romantic love is something one "falls" into. Love is an uncontrollable impulse, and we can only give ourselves over to being at the mercy of its tempest.... Is that it?

YOUTH: Yes, of course. Love does not progress in a calculated way, and it is not something that can be controlled by anyone. And that's why tragedies like *Romeo and Juliet* end up occurring.

PHILOSOPHER: ... All right. I think that what you are talking about now is a view of love that is derived from normal social thinking. But Adler, who doubted the normal thinking of society, shed light from a different angle, and in effect espoused "antitheses to normal social thinking." His opinion with regard to love, for example, was that "love is not, as some psychologists think, a pure and natural function."

YOUTH: ... What's that supposed to mean?

PHILOSOPHER: In short, love to the human being is neither something prescribed by destiny, nor something spontaneously generated. That is to say, we do not "fall" in love.

YOUTH: Then what is it?

PHILOSOPHER: It is something we build. Love that is just "falling," anyone can do. Such a thing is not worthy of being called a life task. It is because we build it up from nothing by our strength of will that the task of love is difficult.

Many people try to speak of love without having any knowledge of this principle. As a result, they must resort to words like "destiny," which is none of our human business, and animalistic "instinct." They avoid looking directly at the task that should be most important to them, as if it were beyond the scope of their will or effort. One may even say that they are not engaging in loving.

YOUTH: They're not engaging in loving!?

PHILOSOPHER: That's right. This is probably also the case for you, who talk of "falling in love." We must think about the human love that is neither divine nor animal.

From an Art of Being Loved
toward an Art of Loving

YOUTH: I could refute that in all kinds of ways. Look, every one of us has been through the experience of falling for someone. I'm sure you are no exception. If you are a human living in this world, you experience again and again that tempest of love, that unstoppable impulse of love. In other words, "falling in love" definitely exists. You'll acknowledge this fact, won't you!?

PHILOSOPHER: Think of it this way. Suppose there is a camera you want. You're fascinated by a German-made, twin-lens reflex camera that you happened to see one day in a shop window. Though you have never touched the camera and don't even know how to focus its lens, you crave to possess it someday. You would carry it with you all the time, and take pictures whenever the spirit moved you. . . . It doesn't have to be a camera. Shoes, a car, a musical instrument—it could be anything. You can imagine the feeling, right?

YOUTH: Yes, I know it well.

PHILOSOPHER: At this time, your obsession with that camera will be just like your falling for someone, and you will be beset by a "tempest" of endless desire. When you close your eyes, its form comes to you, and in the farthest reaches of your ears you can even hear the sound of the shutter—your condition is such that no other thing can enter your head.

If it were during childhood, you might have whined and cried about it to your parents.

YOUTH: . . . Well, sure.

PHILOSOPHER: But when you actually get the camera, you get tired of it not even six months later. Why do you tire of it so soon after finally getting it? It isn't that you wanted to photograph with a German camera. You just wanted to acquire, to possess, and to triumph. . . . The "falling in love" you speak of is no different from this desire to possess, or this desire for triumph.

YOUTH: So, in other words, "falling for someone" is like becoming obsessed with material things?

PHILOSOPHER: Of course, the other party is a living human being, so it should be easy to add in a romantic story. But essentially it is the same as the desire for material things.

YOUTH: . . . Eh, what a masterpiece.

PHILOSOPHER: What's wrong?

YOUTH: . . . What do you know about people anyway? Even as you preach neighborly love, out seeps this ridiculous stew of nihilism! What "human love"? What "antitheses to normal social thinking"? You can take those ideas and feed them to the rats in the sewers!!

PHILOSOPHER: There are probably two points you have misunderstood with regard to the premise of this discussion. The first one is that you are focusing on the story of Cinderella in her glass slippers, up until she gets married to the prince. Adler, on the other hand, is focused on their relationship after they get married, after the closing credits have passed and the movie is over.

YOUTH: Their relationship after they get married?

PHILOSOPHER: Yes. For example, even if their passionate love leads to marriage, that is not the goal of love. Marriage is really the starting point of their love. Because real life will continue, day after day, from that point.

YOUTH: . . . So, the love that Adler talks about is married life?

PHILOSOPHER: Then there is the other point. Adler devoted much of his energy to giving lectures, and apparently the majority of the requests he received from his audience were love-related consultations. There are many psychologists in the world who advocate the "art of being loved by another person." On how to be loved by the person one desires. And that may have been the sort of advice that people were expecting from Adler too.

But the love that Adler spoke of was something completely different. Consistently, he advocated an active art of loving, that is to say, the "art of loving another person."

YOUTH: An art of loving?

PHILOSOPHER: Yes. To understand this way of thinking, one may turn not only to Adler, but to the words of Erich Fromm as well. He even published a book by the same name, *The Art of Loving*, which was a worldwide bestseller.

To be sure, it is difficult to be loved by another person. But loving another person is a task of far greater difficulty.

YOUTH: Who would believe such a joke!? Loving is something any wretch is capable of. The difficult thing is to be loved! It's no exaggeration to say that the anxiety of love is summed up in that phrase!

PHILOSOPHER: I once thought so too. But now that I know Adler, and have put his ideas into practice in child-rearing, and have come to know of the existence of a great love, I hold a view that is the complete opposite. This is an area that touches the core of Adler. . . . When you know the difficulty of loving, you will understand everything about Adler.

Love Is a Task Accomplished
by Two People

YOUTH: No, I am not going to concede! If loving were the only thing, it could be done by anyone. No matter how warped a person's character, no matter how much of a failure they might be, that person has someone they long for. In other words, one can love another person. But being loved by another person is extremely difficult. . . . I'm a fine example. I look like this, and whenever there's a woman in front of me, I blush, my voice turns shrill, and my eyes get jittery. I don't have a good position in society, and not much in terms of finances either. And to make matters worse, I've got this cynical personality. Ha-ha! Who could possibly love someone like me!?

PHILOSOPHER: In your life until now, have you ever loved someone?

YOUTH: . . . Sure, I have.

PHILOSOPHER: Was it easy to love that person?

YOUTH: It's not a question of it being difficult or easy! Before you realize it, you're falling for someone, and then you're in love with that person and can't get them out of your head. That's just the emotion called love!

PHILOSOPHER: And do you love someone now?

YOUTH: . . . No.

PHILOSOPHER: Why is that? It's easy to love, isn't it?

YOUTH: Damn it! Talking to you is like hanging out with a heartless machine! Loving is easy. Without a doubt, it is easy. However, finding the person one should love is difficult!! That's the problem—finding the person one should love!

Once you find the person you should love, the tempest of love will start raging inside you. A violent tempest that there's no way of stopping!

PHILOSOPHER: I see. Love is not a question of "art," but of one's "target." The important thing about love is not *how* one should love, but *whom* one should love. Is that it?

YOUTH: Of course!

PHILOSOPHER: Now, how does Adler define love relationships? Let's go over that.

YOUTH: . . . I'm sure it'll just be another one of his tiresome idealistic theories.

PHILOSOPHER: First, Adler says this: "We receive education on the task that is accomplished on one's own, and on the work that is accomplished by twenty people. But we do not receive education on the task that is accomplished by two people."

YOUTH: . . . The task that is accomplished by two people?

PHILOSOPHER: For example, the baby who could barely even turn over in bed manages to stand up on their own two feet and walk around. This is a "task accomplished on one's own" that they cannot get anyone else to do for them—standing up and walking, learning words and communicating. Moreover, philosophy, mathematics, physics, and every other field of study would qualify as a task accomplished on one's own.

YOUTH: I suppose they would.

PHILOSOPHER: By contrast, work is a "task accomplished with one's comrades." Even with the kind of work that would seem to be undertaken on one's own—for example, that of a painter—there are always cooperators. The people who make the paints and paintbrushes, the people who make the canvases and easels, and then the purchasers at the art dealer. There is no such thing as work that can come into being without connections with other people, and without cooperation.

YOUTH: Yes, that's true.

PHILOSOPHER: And we receive sufficient education in our homes and schools with regard to the tasks that are accomplished on one's own and the tasks that are accomplished with one's comrades. That's how it is, yes?

YOUTH: Well, yes. We teach it properly at our school too.

PHILOSOPHER: The thing is, we receive no education whatsoever on the "task to be accomplished by two people."

YOUTH: And that "task to be accomplished by two people" is . . . ?

PHILOSOPHER: The love that Adler speaks of.

YOUTH: So, love is a task accomplished by two people. But we do not learn the art with which to accomplish that. . . . Is it all right to understand it in this way?

PHILOSOPHER: Yes.

YOUTH: . . . Heh-heh. You realize that I'm not convinced by any of this, don't you?

PHILOSOPHER: Yes, this is nothing more than the gateway. What is love to the human being? What points are different between it and one's work relationships and friend relationships? And then, why do we need to love other people? . . . Dawn is fast approaching. We do not have much time left. Let's think this over together and make every minute count.

Switch the Subject of Life

YOUTH: Then I'll ask you straight out. Love is a "task accomplished by two people." . . . This is an example of pretending to state something while not actually stating anything at all. What on earth do these two people accomplish, anyway?

PHILOSOPHER: Happiness. They accomplish a happy life.

YOUTH: Wow, you answered that right away!

PHILOSOPHER: We all wish to be happy. We live in the pursuit of a happier life. You will agree with that, yes?

YOUTH: Of course.

PHILOSOPHER: And in order to be happy, we have to take steps within our interpersonal relationships. All human problems are interpersonal relationship problems. And all human happiness is interpersonal relationship happiness. I have spoken about this several times before.

YOUTH: Yes. This is exactly why we have to embark on the life tasks.

PHILOSOPHER: Now, concretely speaking, what is happiness to a human being? That time three years ago, I mentioned Adler's conclusion with regard to happiness. In short: "Happiness is the feeling of contribution."

YOUTH: Right. It's a pretty bold conclusion to make.

PHILOSOPHER: As Adler puts it, for all of us, it is only when we can feel "I am of use to someone" that we can have a true awareness that we have worth. We can have a true awareness of our worth and gain the sense of belonging, that "it's okay to be here." But on the other hand, we have no way of knowing whether our conduct is really useful. Because even if there is a person right in front of you who appears to be enjoying things, in principle there is no way you can tell if they are "really" enjoying things.

This brings us to the term "feeling of contribution." All we need is the subjective sense that "I am of use to someone," or in other words, a "feeling of contribution." There is no need to look for any other basis. Try to find happiness in the feeling of contribution. Try to find joy in the feeling of contribution.

We gain a true awareness that we are of use to someone through our work relationships. We gain a true awareness that we are of use to someone through our friend relationships. And if we do that, then happiness is right in front of us.

YOUTH: Yes, I accept that. Frankly speaking, what you are presenting now is the most simply put, and most convincing, of the various theories of happiness I have encountered. And conversely, that is exactly why I can't really get this argument that one can accomplish a "happy life" through love.

PHILOSOPHER: That could be the reason. Then please stop for a moment and recall our discussion regarding division of labor. Lying at the very root of the division of labor was "my happiness," that is to say, self-interest. Ultimately, my happiness in effect connects to someone else's happiness. A division-of-labor relationship is established. In a word, there is a healthy give-and-take at work. That is what we were talking about.

YOUTH: Yes, it's a very interesting discussion.

PHILOSOPHER: On the other hand, the thing that establishes a friend relationship is "your happiness." One has unconditional confidence in the other party, without seeking collateral or anything in return. There is no idea of give-and-take here. It is through an other-interested attitude of wholeheartedly believing and giving that friend relationships come about.

YOUTH: Give, and it shall be given unto you . . . Right?

PHILOSOPHER: Yes. In other words, it is by pursuing "my happiness" that we build division-of-labor relationships, and by pursuing "your happiness" that we build friend relationships. So, what is it that we pursue that allows love relationships to come about?

YOUTH: . . . I guess it'd be the happiness of the person one loves, a lofty "your happiness."

PHILOSOPHER: No, it is not.

YOUTH: Oho! . . . So you're saying that love is really egoism, that is to say, "my happiness"?

PHILOSOPHER: It is not that either.

YOUTH: Then what is it!?

PHILOSOPHER: Rather than the self-interested seeking of "my happiness" or the other-interested wishing for "your happiness," love is the building of a happiness of an inseparable "us."

YOUTH: . . . An inseparable us?

PHILOSOPHER: That's right. One upholds "us" as being higher than "me" or "you." One maintains that order in all of one's choices in life. One does not give precedence to the happiness of "me," and one is not satisfied

223

with only the happiness of "you." Unless it is the happiness of two of "us," it has no meaning. Such is the "task accomplished by two people."

YOUTH: So, it's about being self-interested, while also being other-interested . . . ?

PHILOSOPHER: No. It is *not* self-interested, and it is *not* other-interested either. Love has neither self-interest nor other-interest—it rejects both.

YOUTH: Why?

PHILOSOPHER: . . . Because that changes the "subject of life."

YOUTH: The subject of life!?

PHILOSOPHER: From the time we are born, we go about our lives looking at the world with the eyes of "me," hearing sounds through the ears of "me," and pursuing the happiness of "me." This is so for all people. When one knows real love, however, the subject of life changes from "me" to "us." It allows one to live by completely new guidelines that are of neither self-interest nor other-interest.

YOUTH: But wouldn't that mean that the "me" would vanish into nothingness?

PHILOSOPHER: Indeed. The "me" should vanish into nothingness, if one is to find a happy life.

YOUTH: What did you say!?

Self-Reliance Is Breaking Away from "Me"

PHILOSOPHER: Love is a task accomplished by two people. Through love, two people accomplish a happy life. Then why does love connect to happiness? In short, it is because love is liberation from "me."

YOUTH: Liberation from "me"!?

PHILOSOPHER: Yes. When we are given life in this world, at first we reign supreme at "the center of the world." Everyone in our vicinity worries about "me," soothes us day and night, provides food, and even takes care of our excretions. Whenever "me" smiles, the world smiles too, and when "me" cries, the world hurries to our aid. In most cases, we are in a condition like a dictator who reigns over the household domain.

YOUTH: Well, that's how it is today, at least.

PHILOSOPHER: What is the source of this overwhelming, almost dictatorial power? Adler asserts that it is "weakness." That in childhood, we control the adults by way of our own weakness.

YOUTH: . . . Because we are weak beings, the people in our vicinity have to help us?

PHILOSOPHER: Right. Weakness becomes a frightfully powerful weapon in an interpersonal relationship. This was a crucial discovery that Adler arrived at on the basis of deep insights gained from clinical practice.

Let's use the story of a certain boy as an example. The boy was afraid of the dark. At night, his mother would put him to bed, turn out the light, and leave the room. And every time, he would begin to cry. Since he would not stop crying, his mother would come back and ask him, "Why are you crying?" Once he had settled down, he would answer in a frail voice, "'Cause it's so dark." The mother, having perceived her son's goal, would ask him with a sigh, "So, now that I'm back, is it a little lighter?"

YOUTH: Heh-heh. I'm sure it would be!

PHILOSOPHER: Darkness itself wasn't the problem. The thing that the boy feared and wanted to avoid most of all was being separated from his mother. As Adler puts it, "By crying, calling her, not being able to sleep, or by some other means, he turns himself into a troublemaker, and endeavors to keep his mother near him."

YOUTH: He controls his mother by calling special attention to his weakness.

PHILOSOPHER: That's right. To paraphrase Adler again, "Once, they lived in a golden age in which everything they wanted was given to them. And among them, there are those who will still feel that if they cry enough, protest enough, and refuse to cooperate, they will continue to be able to get whatever they want. They are incapable of focusing on anything aside from their own individual profit, and they cannot see life and society as a whole."

YOUTH: ... A golden age! That's certainly the case—it is a golden age for the children, all right!

PHILOSOPHER: Children are not the only ones who choose such a way of living. There are many adults who treat their own weakness or misfortune, their hurt, troubled background, and trauma, as a weapon, and plot how they will control other people. They will try to control others by making them worry, and by restricting their own words and actions.

Adler referred to such adults as "pampered children," and was very critical of their lifestyle and worldview.

YOUTH: Ah, I can't stand it either. They always think they can fix things by crying, and that laying bare their hurt lets them off the hook. And they regard strong people as "evil" and try to make their weak selves out to be "good"! According to their logic, it's not acceptable for us to get strong, either! Because if you get stronger, it means you've sold your soul to the devil, and fallen into "evil"!

PHILOSOPHER: There is one thing we need to keep in mind here, however, and that is the physical inferiority of the child, in particular of the newborn baby who has just come into this world.

YOUTH: The newborn?

PHILOSOPHER: In principle, children are incapable of self-support. They control the adults around them by crying, that is to say, by calling attention to their own weakness, and if they cannot get the adults to do as they wish them to, they might not last another day. They are not crying because they are pampered or selfish. If they are going to live, they have no choice but to reign supreme at "the center of the world."

YOUTH: . . . Hmm! Undoubtedly.

PHILOSOPHER: All human beings start off with an almost excessive self-centeredness. They would not survive otherwise. However, one cannot reign supreme at the center of the world forever. One has to make peace with the world, and come to the understanding that one is a part of the world. . . . If you are able to comprehend that, then the meaning of the term "self-reliance," which we have discussed numerous times today, should become clear too.

YOUTH: ... The meaning of self-reliance?

PHILOSOPHER: That's right. Why the objective of education is self-reliance. Why Adlerian psychology treats education as one of the most important issues. What meaning is contained in the term "self-reliance"?

YOUTH: Please tell me.

PHILOSOPHER: Self-reliance is "breaking away from self-centeredness."

YOUTH: ... !!

PHILOSOPHER: This is why Adler called community feeling "social interest," and also referred to it as concern for society and concern for others. We have to get past our obstinate self-centeredness and stop trying to be the center of the world. One has to break away from "me." One has to break away from one's pampered childhood lifestyle.

YOUTH: So, when we can break away from self-centeredness, we can achieve self-reliance at last ... ?

PHILOSOPHER: That's right. People can change. We can change that lifestyle, that worldview or outlook on life. And love can change the subject of life from "me" to "us." It is through love that we are liberated from "me," that we achieve self-reliance, and truly accept the world.

YOUTH: Accept the world!?

PHILOSOPHER: Yes. To know love, and to change the subject of life to "us"—this is a new start to life. The "us" that began as just two people will eventually broaden in scope to the entire community, and the entire human race.

YOUTH: That is . . .

PHILOSOPHER: It is community feeling.

YOUTH: . . . Love, self-reliance, and community feeling! Lo and behold, all of Adler's ideas are connected!

PHILOSOPHER: That's right—we are now nearing a major conclusion. Let's go down together to the very depths of the matter.

The "love" that the philosopher had begun talking about was something utterly different from what the youth had been expecting. Love is a "task accomplished by two people," and what we must pursue therein is not the happiness of "me" or the happiness of "you," but the happiness of "us." Only then can we break away from "me" to be liberated from self-centeredness and achieve true self-reliance. To be self-reliant is to break away from one's childhood lifestyle, and to get past one's self-centeredness. In that very moment, the youth had the intuition that he was trying to open a large door. What could be waiting for him on the other side of that door—radiant light, or inky darkness . . . ? All he knew for sure was that he had his hand on the doorknob of his own destiny.

To Whom Is That Love Directed?

YOUTH: ... How deep are those depths?

PHILOSOPHER: When thinking about the relationship between love and self-reliance, the task one cannot avoid addressing is that of the parent-child relationship.

YOUTH: Ah ... I get it, of course, of course.

PHILOSOPHER: Newborns are incapable of living by their own power. It is due to the constant devotion of other people—principally their mothers—that they are eventually able to sustain themselves. We are alive here and now because we had the love of our mothers and fathers, and because there was devotion. The person who thinks, *I was raised without love from anyone,* must not turn away from this fact.

YOUTH: That's true. There was an unsurpassably beautiful, selfless love.

PHILOSOPHER: But if we change the viewpoint, the love here involves a very troublesome matter that cannot be completely settled with the beautiful bond between parent and child.

YOUTH: What could it be?

PHILOSOPHER: No matter how much we reign supreme at the center of the world during childhood, we are dependent on our parents to stay alive.

Our parents have power over the life of this "me," and if we are abandoned by our parents, we will die.

. . . Children are intelligent enough to understand this. And at some point, they realize: *It is because I am loved by my parents that I can go on living.*

YOUTH: . . . Undoubtedly.

PHILOSOPHER: And it is exactly at that point in time that children choose their own lifestyles. What kind of place is this world in which they live, what kind of people inhabit it, and what about the children themselves—what kind of people are they? They choose their "attitudes toward life" of their own accord. . . . Do you understand what this fact means?

YOUTH: N-no, I don't.

PHILOSOPHER: When we choose our lifestyle, its objective can only be to find out "how I can be loved." We all choose a "lifestyle for being loved" as a survival strategy that is directly linked to our lives.

YOUTH: A lifestyle for being loved!?

PHILOSOPHER: Children are excellent observers. They think about the environment in which they have been placed and take measure of the personalities and dispositions of their parents. If they have siblings, they surmise the positional relationships between them, take stock of their personalities, and consider which "me" will be loved; and on the basis of all these aspects, they choose their lifestyle.

For example, at this point, there are children who choose the lifestyle of the "good child" who obeys their parents. And conversely, there are those who choose the lifestyle of the "bad child," who opposes, rejects, and rebels against almost everything.

YOUTH: But why? If they turn into the "bad child," they won't stand a chance of being loved, will they?

PHILOSOPHER: This is a point that is frequently misunderstood. Children who cry, get angry, and shout in rebellion are not incapable of controlling their emotions. Actually, they control their emotions rather too well, and turn them into action. Because they have the intuition that unless they go that far, they will never gain their parents' love and attention, and their very lives will be endangered.

YOUTH: So, that's a survival strategy too!

PHILOSOPHER: That's right. A "lifestyle for being loved" is, in all respects, a self-centered lifestyle of garnering attention from others however possible, and searching out how one can stand, however possible, at the center of the world.

YOUTH: . . . It's all coming together, finally. Briefly put, the various problem behaviors my students engage in are based on that self-centeredness. So, what you are saying is that their problem behavior comes out of their chosen lifestyle for being loved?

PHILOSOPHER: But that's not all. That "how I can be loved," which is rooted in the survival strategies of your childhood, has probably become a criterion of the lifestyle you are adopting now.

YOUTH: What did you say!?

PHILOSOPHER: In the truest sense of the word, you still have not achieved self-reliance. You are still stuck in a lifestyle of being "someone's child." If you want to assist in your students' self-reliance and hope to become a true educator, first you must be self-reliant yourself.

YOUTH: How can you make such assumptions!? And on what grounds? I have entered the teaching profession and I live in that social circle. I have chosen my work of my own accord, I support myself on my own earnings, and I have never asked my parents for money or anything like that. I already am self-reliant!

PHILOSOPHER: But you do not love anyone yet.

YOUTH: . . . Argh!!

PHILOSOPHER: Self-reliance is not an economic issue or a work issue. It is an attitude toward life, an issue of lifestyle. . . . At some point, the time will come when you resolve to love someone. That will be when you achieve separation from your childhood lifestyle and achieve true self-reliance. Because it is through loving others that we at last become adults.

YOUTH: We become adults by loving . . . !?

PHILOSOPHER: Yes. Love is self-reliance. It is to become an adult. That is why love is difficult.

How Can One Get
One's Parents' Love?

YOUTH: But I am self-reliant! I am not reliant on my parents anymore! Wanting to be loved by them never even crosses my mind! Instead of entering the profession my parents had hoped for, I worked for low pay at the university library, and now I am moving forward on the path of the educator. I've resolved to myself that even if this creates rifts in our parent-child relationship, I don't care, and I am ready to be disliked. To me, at the very least, my choice of profession was a way of breaking away from my "childhood lifestyle"!

PHILOSOPHER: . . . You have one sibling, an older brother, am I right?

YOUTH: Yes. My brother is taking over the printing plant that our father runs.

PHILOSOPHER: It seems that following the same path as your family did not sit right with you. The important thing to you was "something different from everyone else." If you went into the same line of work as your father and your brother, you would not be able to garner attention, and you would not be able to realize your own worth.

YOUTH: What? What did you say!?

PHILOSOPHER: But it goes beyond work. From early childhood onward, since your brother was older than you, no matter what you did, he had more power and more experience, and you never had the slightest chance of winning. Now, what could you do about it?

According to Adler, "In general, the youngest child chooses a path that differs completely from the other members of his family. In other words, if it is a family of scientists, he will become a musician or a merchant. If it is a family of merchants, he might become a poet. He must always be different from other people."

YOUTH: That's just an assumption! That is an assumption that makes a mockery of a person's free will!

PHILOSOPHER: Yes. Adler himself only spoke of "tendencies" with regard to sibling birth order. However, it is useful to know what sort of tendencies are brought about by the environment one is placed in.

YOUTH: . . . Then what about my brother? What sort of tendencies does he have?

PHILOSOPHER: For the first-born child, and also for the only child, the greatest privilege may be that one had a "time in which one monopolized one's parents' love." Later-born children do not have the experience of "monopolizing" their parents. They always have a rival who is ahead of them, and in many cases, they are placed in competition relationships.

Yet the first-born child who has monopolized their parents' love, on the birth of a brother or sister will be forced to come down from that position. The first-born child who does not cope with this setback satisfactorily will hope to someday regain that seat of power. Adler refers to this as being a "worshipper of the past" who creates a lifestyle that is conservative, and is pessimistic with regard to the future.

YOUTH: Heh-heh. My brother certainly does have such tendencies.

PHILOSOPHER: It is a lifestyle in which one has a perception of the importance of strength and authority, enjoys wielding one's power, and places excessive value on the rule of law. It is a true conservative lifestyle.

Yet when a brother or sister is born, the first-born child who has already received education with regard to cooperation and assistance is likely to develop into an excellent leader. In imitation of the child-rearing done by the parents, such a first-born finds joy in taking care of siblings and learns the meaning of contribution.

YOUTH: Then what about the second child? In my case, I am the second child, but also the last-born. What sorts of "tendencies" does the second child have?

PHILOSOPHER: Adler says that a typical second child is instantly recognizable. The second child always has a pacesetter running ahead of them. And at the heart of the second child there lies the feeling of "I want to catch up." They want to catch up with their elder brother or sister. To catch up, they have to hurry. They are constantly pushing themselves, and planning how to catch up with, overtake, and even triumph over their elder brother or sister. Unlike the conservative first-born child who holds the rule of law in high regard, the second child wishes to overturn even the natural law of birth order.

So, second children aim for revolution. Rather than trying to be at peace with the existing powers-that-be as first-born children do, they place worth on overthrowing the powers-that-be.

YOUTH: ... You're saying that I've got the tendencies of a rash revolutionary?

PHILOSOPHER: Well, I don't know about that. Because this classification is purely an aid to human understanding—it does not actually determine anything.

YOUTH: Lastly then, what about the only child? Since there are no rivals above or below, the only child gets to always stay in the seat of power?

PHILOSOPHER: It is true that the only child has no siblings who would become rivals. But in this situation, it is the parents who become the rivals. The child wants so much to have his mother's love all to himself that he ends up seeing his father as a rival. He is in an environment that is conducive to the development of the so-called mother complex.

YOUTH: Oh, that's a rather Freudian idea, isn't it?

PHILOSOPHER: But the issue that Adler regarded as more problematic here is the situation of psychological anxiety in which the solitary child is placed.

YOUTH: Psychological anxiety?

PHILOSOPHER: First of all, the child is exposed to the anxiety of always having to look around him, in the worry that a younger brother or sister will be born and that his position will be threatened. More than anything, he lives in fear of the birth of a new prince or a new princess. And beyond that, he needs to watch out for the cowardice of his parents.

YOUTH: The cowardice of his parents?

PHILOSOPHER: That's right. There are couples who, on having one child, tell themselves that "economically speaking, and in terms of the amount of work it would require, there's no way we can afford to raise any more children," and refrain from having any more—regardless of their actual economic situation.

According to Adler, many such couples are cowardly in their lives, and pessimistic. Moreover, anxiety pervades the atmosphere in their homes, and they place an excessive amount of pressure on their only children and make them suffer. As having more than one child was the norm in Adler's time, he laid more emphasis on this point.

YOUTH: . . . So, parents can't just be devoted to loving their children, right?

PHILOSOPHER: Yes. Limitless love so often transforms into a tool for controlling the child. All parents must uphold the clear objective of self-reliance and go about building equal relationships with their children.

YOUTH: And then, regardless of what sort of people their parents are, the children can't help but choose a "lifestyle for being loved."

PHILOSOPHER: That's right. The fact that, in spite of your parents' opposition, you chose to work as a librarian and are now choosing the path of the educator, is not enough on its own to say that you have become self-reliant. Perhaps by choosing a different path, you are actually trying to win the sibling rivalry and keep hold of your parents' attention. And perhaps, by attaining something on that different path, you are hoping to be recognized for your worth as a human being. Perhaps you are attempting to overthrow the existing powers-that-be, and to accede to the throne.

YOUTH: . . . And if that's true, what then?

PHILOSOPHER: You are all caught up in the need for approval. You live thinking about how you can be loved by other people, how you can be recognized by other people. Even the path of the educator, which it would seem you chose yourself, may be a life of "the me that others wish for," a life that has the objective of "being recognized by others."

YOUTH: . . . This path, this life I've chosen as an educator!?

PHILOSOPHER: As long as you hold on to a childhood lifestyle, you will not be able to wipe away that possibility.

YOUTH: Hey, what do you know anyway! I'm just sitting here listening quietly, while you go ahead and fabricate stuff about people's family relationships, and even try to negate me as an educator!

PHILOSOPHER: To be sure, one cannot realize self-reliance by gaining employment. Generally speaking, we live controlled by our parents' love. We choose our lifestyle at a time when we can only crave to be loved by our parents. And further, we grow older and become adults while reinforcing that "lifestyle of being loved."

To get out from under the control of the love one is given, the only thing one can do is love oneself. By loving. Not waiting to be loved or waiting for destiny, but loving someone of one's own accord. That is the only way.

People Are Afraid of Loving

YOUTH: . . . So, even though you usually reduce everything to "courage," this time you're trying to settle it all as being about "love"?

PHILOSOPHER: Love and courage are closely connected. You do not yet know love. You are afraid of love, and you are hesitant about love. Consequently, you are stuck in your childhood lifestyle. You do not have enough courage to dive into love.

YOUTH: I am afraid of love . . . ?

PHILOSOPHER: As Fromm says, "While one is consciously afraid of not being loved, the real, though usually unconscious fear is that of loving." And then he continues by stating, "To love means to commit oneself without guarantee, to give oneself completely. Love is an act of faith, and whoever is of little faith is also of little love."

For example, the moment one has the slightest feeling that the other is showing goodwill toward one, one becomes interested in the other person, and then starts to like them. This kind of thing often happens, doesn't it?

YOUTH: Yes, it does. It would be no exaggeration to say that most love affairs happen that way.

PHILOSOPHER: This is a condition in which one has secured some "guarantee of being loved," even if it is all one's own misunderstanding. One feels some kind of collateral there: "That person probably likes me," or "They probably won't reject my goodwill." And it is on the basis of that collateral that we can begin to love more deeply.

On the other hand, the loving that Fromm speaks of does not provide any such collateral. One loves regardless of what the other person thinks of one. One throws oneself into love.

YOUTH: . . . One must not seek collateral in love.

PHILOSOPHER: Right. Why do people seek collateral in love? Do you know?

YOUTH: They don't want to get hurt or feel miserable. I guess that's why.

PHILOSOPHER: No. Rather, it is that they think, *I'll definitely get hurt.* Or they half-convince themselves: *I'm definitely going to feel miserable.*

YOUTH: What!?

PHILOSOPHER: You do not love yourself yet. You are not able to respect yourself or have confidence in yourself. That is why you end up assuming that in a love relationship you will "definitely get hurt" or "definitely feel miserable." Because you think that there couldn't be anyone who could love someone like you.

YOUTH: . . . But that's just the truth, isn't it!?

PHILOSOPHER: *I am a person without any outstanding traits. That is why I cannot build a love relationship with anyone. I cannot embark on love without collateral.* . . . This is a typical inferiority-complex way of thinking. Because one is using one's feelings of inferiority as an excuse for not resolving one's tasks.

YOUTH: But, but . . .

PHILOSOPHER: One separates the tasks. Loving is your task. But how will the other person respond to your love? That is the other person's task and is not something you can control. What you can do is separate the tasks and love first, from yourself. That is all.

YOUTH: . . . Ah, let's stop for a moment and sort things out. It's true that I have not been able to love myself. I have deep feelings of inferiority, which have developed into an inferiority complex. I have not been able to separate the tasks that need to be separated. Objectively assessing the current discussion, that's about the sum of it.

So, what can I do to dispel my feelings of inferiority? There's only one conclusion. That's to meet a person who will accept and love "this me"! Otherwise, there's no way I can love myself, or anything like that!

PHILOSOPHER: So, in other words, your position is "If you will love me, I will love you"?

YOUTH: . . . Well, I guess so, if you put it briefly.

PHILOSOPHER: So, after all, you are only seeing "Will this person love me?" You seem to be looking at the other person, but you are only seeing yourself. If you are waiting around with such an attitude, who is going to love you?

. . . If there is anyone who would respond to such a self-centered need, it would be one's parents. Because one's parents' love, especially one's mother's love, is unconditional.

YOUTH: . . . You think you can treat me like a child!!

PHILOSOPHER: Listen, that "golden age" is over. And the world is not your mother. You must take a straight look at the childhood lifestyle you have been carrying with you in secret and make it new. Don't wait for someone who will love you to appear.

YOUTH: Ah, we're totally going around in circles!

There Is No Destined One

PHILOSOPHER: We must not stand still. Let us take another step forward. At the outset today, in our discussion concerning education, I spoke of two things that cannot be forced.

YOUTH: . . . Yes, respect and love.

PHILOSOPHER: Right. No matter what sort of dictator I might be, I cannot force people to respect me. In a relationship of respect, the only way is for the respect to come from me first. That is the only thing I can do, regardless of what sort of attitude the other person might take in response. This is what I was talking about earlier.

YOUTH: Then, are you saying that it's the same with love?

PHILOSOPHER: Yes. Love cannot be forced either.

YOUTH: You still haven't answered my main question, however. Look, I do have the feeling of wanting to love someone. In all sincerity, I do. Aside from my fear of love, I have the feeling that I am thirsting for love. Then why don't I launch into love?

. . . It's because I haven't been able to meet that crucial "person one should love"! I haven't been able to meet my destined partner, so my wish for love doesn't come true! The "meeting" is the most difficult problem of all with regard to love!

PHILOSOPHER: So, true love starts with a destined meeting?

YOUTH: But of course it does. Because your partner is someone you devote your life to, and who changes the "subject" of life. You can't pretend you can offer up everything about yourself to just anyone!

PHILOSOPHER: Then, what sort of person would you call a "destined one"? That is to say, how would you sense that it is destiny?

YOUTH: I don't know. . . . I guess I'll know when that time comes. It's unknown territory to me.

PHILOSOPHER: I see. Then let's start by answering with Adler's basic position on this. Whether in love, or in life in general, Adler does not accept the existence of a "destined one" of any kind.

YOUTH: There's no destined one for us!?

PHILOSOPHER: There is not.

YOUTH: . . . Wait, that is not a statement I can just let pass!

PHILOSOPHER: Why do many people seek a destined one in love? Why do we entertain romantic illusions of our marriage partners? The reason, Adler concludes, is "to eliminate all the candidates."

YOUTH: To eliminate the candidates?

PHILOSOPHER: People who lament that they "can't meet anyone," as you do, are actually meeting someone or other on a daily basis. Barring highly unusual circumstances, there is no one who has not met someone in the past year. . . . You have met many people yourself, haven't you?

YOUTH: Well, if you are going to include just being in the same place as them.

247

PHILOSOPHER: However, to grow that modest "meeting" into some kind of "relationship" requires a certain courage. To call out to people, and send letters and such.

YOUTH: Yes, it sure does. It requires not just a certain courage, but the greatest courage of all.

PHILOSOPHER: So, what does a person do when they lose the courage to embark on a relationship? They cling to fantasies of a destined one . . . just like you are doing now.

Even though there often is a person to love right in front of them, they come up with all sorts of reasons to reject each one, and they lower their eyes and think, *There's got to be a more ideal, more perfect, destined partner.* They try not to enter into deeper relationships, and they unilaterally eliminate any and all candidates.

YOUTH: . . . No way.

PHILOSOPHER: By bringing forward excessive and unrealizable ideals in this way, they avoid anything that may lead to interactions with real, living people. Please see that this is the truth of the person who laments that they "can't meet anyone."

YOUTH: I am running away from relationships . . . ?

PHILOSOPHER: And you are living within the realm of possibility. You think of happiness as something that will come from somewhere else: *Happiness hasn't come my way yet, but if I can just meet the person of my destiny, everything will be fine.*

YOUTH: . . . Damn it! Ah, what damn insight you have!

PHILOSOPHER: I am sure that this is not something that feels good to hear. But if you consider the goal of seeking a destined one, the discussion will always come to this point as a matter of course.

Love Is a Decision

YOUTH: Then let's hear it. If there is no destined one, on account of what do we decide to get married? Marriage is making the choice to spend the rest of your life with that one and only person in the whole wide world, isn't it? Surely, you're not saying it's just a matter of choosing according to such "terms" as appearance, finances, and social position, are you?

PHILOSOPHER: Marriage is not a matter of choosing a "target." It is a matter of choosing one's way of living.

YOUTH: Choosing a way of living! Then, the "target" can be anyone?

PHILOSOPHER: Ultimately, yes.

YOUTH: Don't mess around!! Who would ever recognize such a statement? Retract that, retract it right away!!

PHILOSOPHER: I recognize that this is a view that is met with a great deal of opposition. But we are able to love anyone.

YOUTH: I'm not joking! If that's the case, could you just go out and find some woman walking by, without the slightest idea of who she is or where she's from, and love that woman and marry her?

PHILOSOPHER: If I made the decision to do that.

YOUTH: The decision!?

PHILOSOPHER: Of course, there are many people who felt "destiny" on meeting someone and decided to get married in accordance with that intuition. But that is not a previously established destiny. It is only that one decided to believe it was destiny.

As Fromm remarked, "Loving someone is not simply an intense emotion. It is a decision, it is a judgment, it is a promise."

It doesn't matter how the meeting happens, if one makes the firm decision to build real love from that point, and one confronts the "task accomplished by two people." Love is possible with any partner.

YOUTH: . . . Don't you realize? You're spitting on your own marriage right now! You're saying, "My wife wasn't the person of my destiny, and anyone could have been my partner." Would you declare that in front of your family? If you would, then you're an over-the-top nihilist!!

PHILOSOPHER: It is not nihilism—it is realism. Adlerian psychology negates all determinism and rejects fatalism. There is no destined one or anything of the sort for us, and one must not wait for such a person to appear. Nothing will change by having waited. I do not intend to yield on this principle.

However, on looking back on the many years one has journeyed together with one's partner, one may feel the presence of a "destined something" there. Destiny in that case is not a predetermined thing. Nor is it something that has rained down upon one by chance. It should be something that has been built up by the effort of two people.

YOUTH: . . . What do you mean?

PHILOSOPHER: I am sure you understand already. . . . Destiny is something you create with your own two hands.

YOUTH: . . . !!

PHILOSOPHER: We must not become destiny's servants. We must be the masters of our destinies. Rather than seeking a destined person, we build relationships of a kind that might be referred to as destined.

YOUTH: But, concretely speaking, what are you saying one should do?

PHILOSOPHER: One dances. Without thinking about a future one could never comprehend, or about a destiny that could never exist, one simply engages in a dance of the "now" with the partner before one.

Adler recommended dancing to many people, including children, as a "pastime of two human beings taking part in cooperative work." Love and marriage are indeed akin to the dance that two people make together. Without ever thinking about where one would like to go, they take each other by the hand and, looking straight at the happiness of the day that is today, at just this moment called "now," they keep on dancing round and round. People will speak of the tracks of the long dance you two have created as "destiny."

YOUTH: Love and marriage are the dance that two people make together. . . .

PHILOSOPHER: You are standing now at the edge of the dance floor of life and watching other people dance. You are assuming that "there couldn't be anyone who would dance with someone like me," while in your heart you are waiting impatiently for your "destined one" to reach their hand out to you. You are doing everything you can to endure and to protect yourself, so that you do not feel any more miserable than you do already, and so that you do not begin to dislike yourself.

. . . There is one thing that you should do. Take the hand of the person beside you and try to do the best dance that you can possibly do in that moment. Your destiny will start from there.

Re-Choose Your Lifestyle

YOUTH: The guy watching at the edge of the dance floor ... Ha-ha, as usual, you treat people like they're old rags. . . . The thing is, I have tried to do the dance, of course—I have actually tried dancing. I mean, I have been with someone who could be called a lover.

PHILOSOPHER: Yes, I am sure you have.

YOUTH: But it wasn't the kind of relationship that could have ever led to marriage. Both for me and for her, we weren't together to love each other—it was just that we wanted to be able to say that I was her "boyfriend" and she was my "girlfriend." Both of us understood well enough that it was a relationship that would come to an end at some point. We never once talked about our future together, let alone getting married. It was a passing relationship.

PHILOSOPHER: In the days of our youth, we do have such relationships.

YOUTH: Moreover, I regarded her as a compromise from the start. I told myself, "I've got various complaints, but I'm not in the position to aim higher. With her, I'll be living within my means." I think that she probably chose me for the same kind of reason. Well, thinking about it now, it's a pretty embarrassing way of thinking. Even if it was true that I couldn't aim higher.

PHILOSOPHER: It is a great thing that you have been able to face that feeling.

YOUTH: Then, I really want to ask you this: What was it that made you resolve to get married? No destined one or whatever exists, and there's no telling what'll happen to you in the future. There's always the possibility that someone more attractive will come along. If you get married, that possibility disappears. But then, how do we—actually, I mean you—how did you resolve to get married to "this person" and no one else?

PHILOSOPHER: I wanted to be happy.

YOUTH: Huh?

PHILOSOPHER: If I loved this person, I could be happier. That's what I thought. Looking back on it now, I realize that it was a mentality of seeking an "our happiness" that went beyond "my happiness." I did not know about Adler at the time, however, and I had never given any reasoned thought to love and marriage. I only wanted to be happy. That is all.

YOUTH: Well, me too! Everyone gets together in hopes of being happy. But surely that's a different thing from marriage!

PHILOSOPHER: . . . But your hope was not "to be happy," was it? It was simply the desire for things "to be easier."

YOUTH: . . . What!?

PHILOSOPHER: Awaiting a love relationship is not free of difficulty. The responsibility one must take on is great, and painful things and unforeseeable hardships may lie ahead. Is one still capable of loving, in the face of that? Does one have the resolve, no matter what troubles arise, to love this person and walk beside them? Can one make that feeling into a promise?

YOUTH: The responsibility . . . of love?

PHILOSOPHER: Suppose, for example, a person who says, "I like flowers," but lets them wither right away. This person forgets to water them, doesn't think of transplanting them into a different pot or adjusting the amount of light, and just puts the flowerpot in a place where they look nice. To be sure, it may be true that the person likes looking at flowers. But one could not say that this person "loves flowers." Love is a more dedicated approach.

It is the same with you. You were avoiding the responsibility that should be shouldered by the one who loves. You just devoured the fruit of your passion, without watering the flowers or planting the seeds. That is truly a fleeting, hedonistic love.

YOUTH: . . . I know it! I didn't love her! I just took advantage of her good intentions!

PHILOSOPHER: It is not that you didn't love her. You didn't know what "loving" was. If you had known, I am sure you would have been able to build a relationship of destiny with that woman.

YOUTH: With her? I could have, with her!?

PHILOSOPHER: As Fromm says, "Love is an act of faith, and whoever is of little faith is also of little love." Adler, in place of this "faith," would use the word "courage." You were of little courage. So, you were able to love only a little. Not possessing the courage to love, you tried to stay in the lifestyle of your childhood, the lifestyle of being loved. That is all.

YOUTH: With the courage to love, she and I could have . . .

PHILOSOPHER: . . . Yes. The courage to love, that is to say, the "courage to be happy."

YOUTH: You're saying that if I'd had the courage to be happy back then, I could have loved her, and faced the task accomplished by two people?

PHILOSOPHER: And you would have achieved self-reliance.

YOUTH: . . . No, no, I don't get it! Because is it just: "Love is all"? Is love really the only way we can find happiness!?

PHILOSOPHER: Love is all. The person who lives wanting an easy life or looking for the easy way may find fleeting pleasures, but they will not be able to grasp real happiness. It is only by loving another person that we are liberated from self-centeredness. It is only by loving another person that we can achieve self-reliance. And it is only by loving another person that we arrive at community feeling.

YOUTH: But didn't you say before that happiness is a feeling of contribution, and that "if one has a feeling of contribution, one can find happiness"? Was that a lie!!?

PHILOSOPHER: It is not a lie. The issue here is one's method for gaining a feeling of contribution, or rather, one's way of living. By nature, a person should be able to contribute to someone just by being there. One is already contributing by one's "being," not by "acts" that can be seen. There is no need to do anything special.

YOUTH: That's a lie! There's no way to really feel such a thing!

PHILOSOPHER: That is because you are living with "me" as the subject. When you know love, and live with "us" as the subject, that will change. You will gain the real feeling of an "us" that includes the entire human race, in which people are contributing to each other simply by living.

YOUTH: ... I will gain a real feeling of an "us" that includes not only my partner, but the entire human race?

PHILOSOPHER: In other words, you will gain community feeling.... Well, I cannot enter any further into your tasks. But if you were to ask my advice, I would probably say something like this: "Love, be self-reliant, and choose life."

YOUTH: Love, be self-reliant, and choose life!

PHILOSOPHER: ... Look. The eastern sky has begun to lighten.

The youth now understood with his entire being the love described by Adler. *If I have the "courage to be happy," I will be able to love someone, and I will re-choose my life. I'll achieve true self-reliance.* The thick fog that had been clouding his vision was clearing before him. But the youth did not know yet that awaiting him beyond the clearing fog was not some beautiful Eden-like meadow. That to love, be self-reliant, and choose life would be a difficult path.

Keeping It Simple

YOUTH: . . . That's some conclusion.

PHILOSOPHER: Let's wrap things up here. And let's make tonight our final meeting.

YOUTH: Huh?

PHILOSOPHER: This study is not a place where young people like you visit again and again. And more important, you are an educator. The place you should be is in the classroom, and the comrades you should be speaking with are the children who will live in the future.

YOUTH: But I haven't figured things out yet! If we just stop here, I'll definitely lose my way. Because I haven't made it to Adler's stairway yet!

PHILOSOPHER: . . . It's true that you have not begun climbing the stairway. But you have made it to the point where you have a foot on the first step. Three years ago, I said, "The world is simple, and life is too." And now that we have finished our discussion today, I will supplement it with a few more words.

YOUTH: And they are . . . ?

PHILOSOPHER: That the world is simple, and life is too. But also, "Keeping it simple is difficult." It is there that the passage of "nothing days" becomes one's trial.

YOUTH: Ah . . . !!

PHILOSOPHER: Knowing about Adler, being in agreement with Adler, and accepting Adler are not enough to change one's life. People often say that the first step is crucial. That everything will be fine if you just get past it. Of course, it is true that the biggest turning point is the first step.

In real life, however, the trials of "nothing days" begin only after one has embarked on that first step. What is really being tested is one's courage to keep walking on one's path. Just as it is in philosophy.

YOUTH: It's really so—it's really those days that are a trial!

PHILOSOPHER: You are likely to run into conflicts with Adler on many occasions. You will have doubts. You may want to stop walking, and you may tire of loving and want to seek a life of being loved. And you may want to visit this study again.

But at that time, please talk with the children, with your comrades who will live in the coming era. And if you are able, rather than simply inheriting Adler's ideas just as they are, please go about updating them yourselves.

YOUTH: We should update Adler!?

PHILOSOPHER: Adler did not hope for his psychology to become didactically fixed in place and passed down only among specialists. His hope was that his psychology would be positioned as a "psychology for everyone" and continue to thrive, far from the world of academia, as a common sense of the people.

We are not a religion endowed with eternal scriptures. And Adler is not our sacred founder, but a philosopher who existed on the same level as us. . . . Times change. New arts are born, new relationships and new worries also. The common sense of the people undergoes a slow transformation in tandem with the changing times. It is precisely because we value Adler's ideas that we must continue to update them. We must not turn into fundamentalists. This is the mission entrusted to the human beings who will live in the new era.

To the Friends Who Will
Make a New Era

YOUTH: . . . But what about you—what will you do from now on?

PHILOSOPHER: I suppose that other young people who catch wind of me will come. Because no matter how the times change, people's worries stay the same. . . . Please remember: The time we are given is limited. And as our time is limited, all our interpersonal relationships come into being on the premise of our "parting." This is not a nihilistic term—the reality is that we meet in order to part.

YOUTH: . . . Yes, undoubtedly.

PHILOSOPHER: And so, there is one thing we can do: devote our ceaseless efforts, in all our meetings and all our interpersonal relationships, toward the "best possible parting." That is all.

YOUTH: Our ceaseless efforts toward the best possible parting!?

PHILOSOPHER: One devotes one's ceaseless efforts so that when the day of parting comes, one will be able to be satisfied that "meeting this person, and passing the time together with this person, was not a mistake." Whether it is in one's relationship with one's students, in one's relationship with one's parents, or in one's relationship with the person one loves.

If, for example, your relationship with your parents came to an end all of a sudden, or a relationship with a student or a friend came to an end, would you be able to accept it as the "best possible parting"?

YOUTH: N-no. That's so . . .

PHILOSOPHER: Then you have no choice but to start building now the kind of relationship that would make you feel that way. That is what is meant by "live earnestly here and now."

YOUTH: It's not too late? It won't be too late if I start now?

PHILOSOPHER: It is not too late.

YOUTH: But it takes time to put Adler's ideas into practice. You even told me so yourself: "One needs half the number of years one has lived"!

PHILOSOPHER: Yes. But that is the view of an Adlerian researcher. Adler himself said something completely different in this regard.

YOUTH: What did he say?

PHILOSOPHER: In response to the question "Is there a time limit for a person to change?" Adler replied, "Yes, there certainly is a time limit." And then, with a mischievous smile, he added, "Until the day before you meet your maker."

YOUTH: . . . Ha-ha! Some friend!

PHILOSOPHER: Let's embark on love. And devote our ceaseless efforts toward the "best possible parting" with that person we have loved. There is no need to worry about time limits or anything like that.

YOUTH: Do you think it is something I can do? Devote my ceaseless efforts?

PHILOSOPHER: Of course. Ever since we met three years ago, we have been devoting ourselves to those efforts. And now, in this way, we are approaching our best possible parting. We should have no regrets for our time together.

YOUTH: . . . No, none at all!

PHILOSOPHER: I am proud to be able to part while having such a refreshing feeling. To me, you are the best possible friend. Thank you very much.

YOUTH: Oh, well, of course, I am thankful too. I am thankful to hear that, I really am. But I'm not confident that I am a person who is worthy of those words! Is it really necessary to part forever here? Can't we ever meet again?

PHILOSOPHER: It is your independence, your self-reliance as a lover of wisdom, that is to say, as a philosopher. Didn't I say it three years ago? That the answers should not be something you get from someone else, but something you arrive at on your own. You are ready to do that.

YOUTH: Independence, from you . . .

PHILOSOPHER: I have gained a great hope today. Your students will graduate, love someone someday, achieve self-reliance, and become true adults. And one day, there will be dozens, even hundreds of such students, and maybe the times will catch up with Adler.

YOUTH: . . . That is truly the objective I had in mind three years ago, when I set forth on the path of education!

PHILOSOPHER: You are the one who will make that future. There is no hesitating. We cannot see the future because there are infinite possibilities, and that is precisely why we can become the masters of our destinies.

YOUTH: It's true, I can't see a thing ahead of me! Nothing at all—it's almost refreshing!

PHILOSOPHER: I have never once accepted disciples, and in all my interactions with you I have been very careful not to have any awareness of you as a disciple. But now that I have conveyed to you everything that needed to be conveyed, I have the feeling that I have understood something at last.

YOUTH: And what would that be?

PHILOSOPHER: What I have been searching for is not disciples or successors, but a running partner. You will probably encourage me along my path, as an irreplaceable running partner who upholds the same ideals as me. From now on, wherever you are, I am sure I will continue to feel your presence close by.

YOUTH: . . . Yes, I will run! I will run beside you, always!!

PHILOSOPHER: Well, it is time to raise your head and go back to the classroom. The students are waiting. And a new era is waiting for all of you.

The philosopher's study, separated from the outside world. *One step outside that door, chaos awaits me. Noise and discord and unending everyday life await me.*

"The world is simple, and life is too. But keeping it simple is difficult, and it is there that the passage of 'nothing days' becomes one's trial." *It's true—there's no two ways about it. But I'm going to throw myself into the chaos again, regardless. Because my comrades, my students, are living in the midst of great chaos. Because that is the place where I live.*

... The youth took a deep breath and, with grim determination, opened the door.

Afterword

This volume is the sequel to *The Courage to Be Disliked*, which was cowritten with Mr. Ichiro Kishimi and published in 2013.

There were no plans to write a sequel at the outset. Maybe our book did not convey everything about Alfred Adler, but it was a success in its distilling of the essence of his thought. *The Courage to Be Disliked* generated a favorable response, and I could not really see the significance of writing a continuation for a book that already had its conclusion.

Then, one day about a year after the publication of that book, in the midst of a chat about trivial matters, Mr. Kishimi let slip the following words:

"If Socrates and Plato were alive today, they might have chosen the path of psychology, instead of that of philosophy."

Socrates and Plato would have become psychiatrists?

The ideas of Greek philosophy could be brought into a clinical setting?

I was so taken aback, I could not speak for a moment. Mr. Kishimi is the foremost specialist in Adlerian psychology in Japan, and is a philosopher with enough of a familiarity with ancient Greece to be able to handle the translation of Plato. So it was not a statement that made light of Greek philosophy, of course. If I were to specify one thing that led to the making of *The Courage to Be Happy*, I suppose it would have to be this particular comment from Mr. Kishimi.

Adlerian psychology addresses all manner of life problems in plain language that can be understood by anyone, without ever making use of obscure terminology of any kind. It is a form of thought endowed with qualities more akin to philosophy than to psychology. It seems to me that *The Courage to Be Disliked* was widely accepted as a life philosophy, rather than as a book on psychology.

On the other hand, doesn't this philosophical quality actually reveal the incompleteness of Adler's thought as a psychology, and point to its flaws as a science? Isn't that why Adler became a "forgotten giant"? Isn't the very fact that it is not complete as a psychology the reason it did not take root in the academic world? I had interacted with Adler's thought without ever ridding myself of such doubts.

In the end, it was Mr. Kishimi's statement that shed light on them.

Adler did not choose psychology in order to analyze the human mind. Inspired to set off on the path of medicine on the occasion of his younger brother's death, the core matter of his thought was always "What is happiness to the human being?" And at the beginning of the twentieth century, when Adler was alive, the most advanced approach to learning about human beings, and to inquiring into the true form of happiness, just happened to be psychology. One must not fall under the spell of the name "Adlerian psychology," or spend too much time comparing him to Freud and Jung. Had Adler been born in ancient Greece, he might well have chosen philosophy, and had Socrates and Plato been born in our time, they might have chosen psychology. . . . As Mr. Kishimi often says, "Adlerian psychology is a way of thinking that follows in the same vein as Greek philosophy." At long last, I feel that I can grasp the meaning of these words.

And so, after a thorough rereading of Adler's writings as "philosophy texts," I visited Mr. Kishimi's home in Kyoto once again, and we engaged in a lengthy dialogue. Naturally, the main subject of our discussion was happiness theory. It is that question consistently posed by Adler: "What is happiness to a human being?"

Our dialogue, which became even more impassioned than the previous time, explored education theory, organizational theory, work theory, social theory, and even extended to life theory before reaching its conclusion with the grand themes of "love" and "self-reliance." How will the reader take in the love and the self-reliance Adler speaks of? If the reader can feel, as I did, a great astonishment and hope of the sort that sends shock waves through one's entire life, I would know no greater joy.

Lastly, I would like to convey my heartfelt gratitude to Mr. Ichiro Kishimi, who always tackled things head-on as the wisdom-loving philosopher he is; to our editors Yoshifumi Kakiuchi and Diamond Inc.'s Kenji Imaizumi, who gave their steadfast support throughout the lengthy writing period; and most of all, to all our readers.

Thank you very much.

Fumitake Koga

Alfred Adler was an oft-misunderstood thinker for many years.

With his "encouragement" approach in particular, there were innumerable instances of it being presented, or even abused, for purposes that could not be further removed from his original intentions. That is to say, it was used "to control and manipulate other people" in child-rearing and school education settings, as well as in human resource development settings in corporations and the like.

This may be related to the fact that, compared to other psychologists of his time, Adler was passionate about "education." Deeply interested in socialism while at university, after experiencing the realities of the Russian revolution after World War I, Adler lost hope in Marxism. Thereafter, he sought the salvation of the human race not through political reform, but through educational reform.

One of Adler's greatest achievements was the establishment of numerous child guidance clinics, the first in the world in public schools, under the aegis of the city of Vienna.

Furthermore, he used these child guidance clinics not only for providing treatment to children and their parents, but as places for training teachers, doctors, and counselors. In essence, it was from there that Adlerian psychology spread, from its start in schools, to the world.

To Adler, education was not something on the level of raising scholastic achievement, or reforming problem children, or that sort of thing. It was for moving the human race forward and changing the future. *That* was education to him. Adler goes so far as to declare:

"The teacher molds the minds of children and holds the future of mankind in his hands."

Then, did Adler have such expectations only for those in the teaching profession?

No, he did not. As is evident from his characterization of counseling as "reeducation," for Adler, all people living in a community were engaged with education, and all people were in the position of receiving education. I, too, having first encountered Adler through child-rearing, have actually gained a great deal of "human knowledge" from children. Of course, you too must be both an educator and a student.

Regarding his psychology, Adler stated, "Understanding a human being is no easy matter. Of all the forms of psychology, individual psychology is probably the most difficult to learn and put into practice."

One cannot change anything just by studying Adler.

One will make no progress whatsoever just by knowing it as knowledge.

And though one may have gathered one's courage and taken the first step, it won't do if one stops there. Take the next step, and then the next step after that.

Map and compass in hand, what sort of path will you walk from now on? Or will you stay in place? If this book can be of some help in gaining the "courage to be happy," nothing would give me more joy.

Ichiro Kishimi